WITNESS

────◆─◆◆────

WINNER OF THE NATIONAL JEWISH BOOK AWARD — BIOGRAPHY

AN INDIE NEXT LIST PICK

A *PUBLISHERS LUNCH* BUZZ BOOK

"A beautiful, deeply moving memoir . . . [a] complex, multilayered book . . . Burger's honest depiction of doubt — both Wiesel's and his own — is a great strength of this memoir, and its constant concern with the limited power of the individual is timeless. While Wiesel privately worried about the power of one person's words in the face of hatred, this book of questions and memories makes a case for the power of teaching, and for words as perhaps the ultimate teachers of how to live." — *CHICAGO TRIBUNE*

"Burger transports the reader to those salons of learning on the Charles River, where Wiesel's students over the years ranged from the granddaughter of a Nazi SS officer to a Korean minister in training . . . Burger's tone and execution are exactly what his title promises — and in keeping with the way Wiesel lived his life." — *USA TODAY*

"Any reader of *Witness* can now become another student of Wiesel's, and another witness, as it is clear that Ariel Burger has become a teacher with its publication." — *TABLET*

"Inspiring and substantive . . . An insightful and winsome love letter—and, for newcomers to Wiesel, a good introduction."

— *KIRKUS REVIEWS*

"Current, former, and future educators will love the glimpses into Wiesel's practices . . . Burger's love for Wiesel, both professional and personal, shines through, and the reader will walk away with renewed admiration for this remarkable scholar, writer, survivor, and teacher."

— *PUBLISHERS WEEKLY*

"A student of Wiesel's, Burger recounts how Wiesel lit his mind on fire . . . Readers will find their own preconceptions called into question, as though they were in class, too."

— *BOOKLIST*

"Burger, a compassionate heart, fiery soul, and sharp religious mind in his own right, presents a personal side of Wiesel that we normally didn't see . . . We owe Rabbi Dr. Ariel Burger our gratitude for this special opportunity."

— *JEWISH JOURNAL*

"Thought-provoking . . . In the vein of *Tuesdays with Morrie*, Burger shows that Wiesel, a Holocaust survivor and Nobel Peace Prize recipient, was not only an extraordinary human being, but a master teacher."

— *NAPERVILLE* MAGAZINE

"Offers enduring insights for today's struggles . . . The book focuses on one of the central principles of Wiesel's life and teaching: that great books, great philosophers, great literature—the big, enduring questions—can help us with the urgencies of day-to-day living."

— *BU TODAY*

"Burger recounts his inspiring relationship with Wiesel and the generous lessons he learned from him in this hopeful book."

— *BOOKPAGE*

"Burger vividly situates the reader inside Wiesel's classroom. He shares details of the thought-provoking lectures as well as the heartfelt questions with which Wiesel challenged his students."

— *JEWISH BOSTON*

"For health communicators, pharma executives, scientists, physicians, providers, and payers interested in learning how to calibrate their own ethical compass, [*Witness*] is one to place at the top of our reading lists. *Witness* is a moral education — 'a primer on educating against indifference, on the urgency of memory and individual responsibility' . . . It is a guide for ethical behavior and should instill courage in the reader to make tough, necessary decisions."

— *MM&M*

"This book is beautiful and brilliant. The substance of Elie Wiesel's teaching will always be with us. Now, thanks to Ariel Burger — a writer of great spiritual and intellectual integrity — we have access to the *way* Wiesel taught generations of students, not only through his words but in the way he lived his life and held his relationships. Wiesel was a treasure of true humanity in the face of unspeakable suffering. This book is also a treasure, giving us clue after clue about how to transcend and transform the suffering of our own time, turning death into life."

— PARKER J. PALMER, AUTHOR OF
ON THE BRINK OF EVERYTHING, HEALING THE HEART OF DEMOCRACY, AND *THE COURAGE TO TEACH*

"Elie Wiesel became the conscience for a world that had lost its moorings. In *Witness*, we are invited to experience an extraordinary yet mostly unseen dimension of this great figure — Elie Wiesel as teacher. This profoundly personal account from one of his closest students brings a great and mythic being down to earth. Read this book and become a better person."

— RABBI IRVING GREENBERG,
AUTHOR OF *THE JEWISH WAY*

"When Elie Wiesel spoke, the world listened. His voice and words were crucial in the worldwide fight against terror, persecution, and genocide. Ariel Burger gives readers a unique chance to hear Wiesel's private voice, the voice of the caring and loving teacher. Burger takes us behind the scenes and we are better for it."

— DEBORAH E. LIPSTADT, AUTHOR OF
ANTISEMITISM HERE AND NOW

"A beautiful memoir about a master teacher. In *Witness*, Ariel Burger turns us all into Elie Wiesel's students. Readers will enjoy this book so much, they might not even realize how much they're learning from it. Bravo." — DR. RUTH WESTHEIMER,
AUTHOR OF *THE DOCTOR IS IN*

WITNESS

WITNESS

———●●———

Lessons from
Elie Wiesel's Classroom

ARIEL BURGER

Mariner Books
Houghton Mifflin Harcourt
BOSTON   NEW YORK

Library of Congress Cataloging-in-Publication Data

Names: Burger, Ariel, author.

Title: Witness : lessons from Elie Wiesel's classroom / Ariel Burger.

Description: Boston ; New York : Houghton Mifflin Harcourt, 2018. |

Identifiers: LCCN 2018006868 (print) | LCCN 2018008780 (ebook) |

ISBN 9781328804075 (ebook) | ISBN 9781328802699 (hardback) |

ISBN 9780358108528 (paperback)

Subjects: LCSH: Wiesel, Elie, 1928–2016. | Authors, French — 20th century —

Biography. | Holocaust survivors — Biography. | Holocaust, Jewish (1939–1945) —

Study and teaching. | Holocaust, Jewish (1939–1945) — Influence. | Holocaust,

Jewish (1939–1945) — Moral and ethical aspects. | BISAC: RELIGION /

Judaism / General. | EDUCATION / Philosophy & Social Aspects. |

PHILOSOPHY / Movements / Humanism.

Classification: LCC PQ2683.132 (ebook) | LCC PQ2683.132 Z598 2018 (print) |

DDC 848/.91409 — dc23

LC record available at https://lccn.loc.gov/2018006868

Book design by Margaret Rosewitz

Printed in the United States of America

DOC 10 9 8 7 6 5 4 3 2 1

Frontispiece photo by Kalman Zabarsky for Boston University Photography

Text permissions appear on page 267.

This is a work of creative nonfiction. The events are portrayed to the best of my memory. While all the stories in this book are true, some names and identifying details have been changed to protect the privacy of the people involved.

For Ness, Yaakov, Yovel, Menachem;
and for Elijah and Shira

Contents

A Note to the Reader

THIS BOOK IS BASED on twenty-five years' worth of journal entries, five years of classroom notes, and interviews with Elie Wiesel's students from all over the world. The classroom notes were taken in shorthand in my terrible handwriting, which I sometimes had trouble deciphering.

In addition to my written notes, after I bought my first smartphone (in 2007), every time I met with Professor Wiesel, I left his office and recorded notes on a voice memo. These recordings gave me a window into the content of many of our conversations and reminded me of how I felt upon leaving him. Listening now, I can hear my excitement as I walked up Bay State Road in Boston or Madison Avenue in New York City. I spoke quickly, trying hard not to forget anything.

Recently I found some cards with Professor Wiesel's scrawled notes in blue ink in my copies of Goethe's *Faust,* Ismail Kadare's *Elegy for Kosovo,* and Bertolt Brecht's *Mother Courage and Her Children,* all books we were reading in class. His handwriting is difficult to read but I include some of those notes in the book.

And I had the privilege and pleasure of connecting with several of his former close students, who were generous with their time and stories. They shared many of the moments from the classroom that you will encounter in this book as well as their current reflections, shaped by the intervening years, on what it was like to be Professor Wiesel's student. I am grateful to them for sharing their memories.

Introduction

ELIE WIESEL IS BEST KNOWN for his Holocaust testimony and for the universal lessons he drew from his particular experience of tragedy. Author of *Night,* which has become part of the modern canon and is taught in high schools across the globe, and winner of the Nobel Peace Prize, Wiesel worked tirelessly on behalf of suffering people everywhere. Over decades, he traveled to Cambodia, Bosnia, Moscow, South Africa, and many other places to protest oppression and to bear witness for victims in an effort to let them know they were not alone. He was a writer, witness, and human rights activist, "a towering moral figure," in the words of Krista Tippett.

But if you asked him, as several interviewers did over the years, what he saw as the core of his life's mission, his answer was always the same: teaching. He often said, "I am a teacher first, and teaching is the last thing I will give up." He saw his writing as an extension of this role, and his activism as its public face. In one of his memoirs he wrote, "In Boston my students gave me joy and vice versa . . . I learn along with my students . . . I could stop, I don't . . . Teaching requires all one's energy, all one's attention, all the curiosity I have. I have no other métier. And I am not looking for one."

I was Elie Wiesel's student, and although he died in July of 2016, I still am. For five years I served as his teaching assistant while pursuing a doctorate at Boston University. I worked with him closely, choosing course topics, planning syllabi and readings, leading discussion sections. In those classes I witnessed his exceptional approach to education. It was academically rigorous, yet welcomed students' searches for personal meaning. It was rooted in classical intellectual and literary traditions, yet spoke directly to the most contemporary concerns. It took place in a secular university but comfortably employed religious and theological language. It was, in short, a rare thing: a humanities education designed to produce morally responsible, sensitive, justice-seeking humanists. Over the years, I saw hundreds of students transformed.

But I was his student well before I served alongside him in the classroom; I was his student since the moment I met him, at age fifteen. He was my mentor, my guide, and eventually my friend. He helped me steer my way through complex questions of identity, religion, and vocation to a life of meaning I did not know was possible.

Over twenty-five years, we spent many hours together talking about personal and political matters, our childhoods, biblical stories and commentaries, art, music, faith. I asked him for advice about career decisions, parenting, and marriage. He often responded with other questions for me to ponder rather than answers or specific directives. Yet somehow his questions helped me clarify my own. Because of him, I became something greater than any role I'd imagined for myself. I became a teacher.

Elie Wiesel believed in the power of education to change history. He saw the simple act of transmission from teacher to student as a source of hope as the world continued to struggle with itself. We wish for peace, justice, and we know that we need to heal ourselves and our planet, but things seem to be getting worse. We feel overwhelmed and don't know how we can intervene even if we had the strength. We struggle to nurture our inner lives in a noisy time, and faith, any sort of faith, often seems far away. We need compelling moral voices, models of integrity, and they are hard to find.

Elie Wiesel is one such voice, a man whose life experience led him on a quest for knowledge, understanding, and sensitivity. Wiesel was a student when, in May 1944, he was deported with his family to Auschwitz. His mother and younger sister were murdered upon arrival. Elie and his father endured forced labor and then a forced march to Buchenwald, where his father died. American soldiers liberated the camp on April 29, 1945. Elie was sixteen.

After the war, he continued his studies and became a journalist. In 1956 he published his first book, *Night,* about his experiences during the Holocaust. He began giving talks on classical and modern philosophical, religious, and literary themes, and in 1972 he was invited to teach at City College of New York. In 1976 he moved to Boston University, which he came to see as his intellectual home, and where he taught for the next thirty-four years.

At BU, Professor Wiesel offered two courses in the fall semester of every year. One was taught on Mondays and was devoted to a broad philosophical or literary theme, like faith and heresy or literary responses to oppression; the Tuesday classes focused on a seminal religious text—the book of Genesis, the book of Job, or a classic work of Hasidic thought. Among the courses he taught over the years were Parable and Paradox; Conflict and Confrontation: Coping with God; Suicide in Literature; The Master/Disciple Relationship in Ancient and Modern Literature; Franz Kafka's Exile and Memory; Writers on Writing; Literature of Prison; and Hidden Literature and Banned Books. Each lecture was preceded and followed by discussion sections led by his teaching assistants in which we reviewed the assigned reading (students read a book each week) and explored the themes brought up in class.

Professor Wiesel often spoke of his respect for his students in his public lectures, which were large and imposing events attended by over three thousand people. He would say, with a twinkle in his eye, "Every year I say that my students this year are the best I've ever had, and every year I am right. But *this* year they really are the best!" This sentiment was expressed in the class structure; he decided early on that his classes would begin with the students' voices, not his. Two students spoke for ten minutes on each week's reading. Most of these were straightforward presentations, but occasionally they were artistic, as when a student performed an interpretive dance to convey the feeling of a work. Professor Wiesel's lecture usually began with his response to the questions his students had raised.

In the pages that follow, I open an intimate window into Elie Wiesel's classroom. We will explore some of the central themes to which he returned again and again in his life and teaching, including topics that you may not immediately associate with Elie Wiesel, for he was obsessed not only with the Holocaust and human rights, but with memory, faith and doubt, madness and rebellion.

So let us settle into the classroom where Professor Wiesel is about to give the first lecture of the semester. The students, who have been shuffling papers and conversing quietly, fall silent. The silence fills the room as light from the morning sun filters through the classroom's high windows. Wiesel stands behind an old wooden chair and says a simple "Good morning," and the class responds in kind.

He smiles and says, "Let us begin with *your* questions."

I
Memory

Listening to a witness makes you a witness.

— ELIE WIESEL

What Can Save Us?

ON A COLD DECEMBER MORNING in 2005 in Boston, Elie Wiesel stands before a classroom full of students. They are local and international students, undergrads, future PhDs, auditing retirees, and professionals pursuing midcareer second degrees. It is the final meeting of Professor Wiesel's weekly course, and students have the floor. In this last class, unlike all the others, they are invited to ask him anything they'd like, even if their questions do not relate directly to the course topic. Tensions in the Middle East have flared again, and students are eager to hear his perspective on prospects for peace. He speaks for half an hour about the political realities, which he connects to the course readings — literature and current events as commentary on each other.

When he finishes, Rachel, a doctoral student and a granddaughter of Holocaust survivors, raises her hand and asks a question. "Professor, what kept you going after the Holocaust? How did you not give up?"

Professor Wiesel answers immediately: "Learning. Before the war, I was studying a page of Talmud, and my studies were interrupted. After the war, when I arrived at the orphanage in France, my first request was for that same volume so that I could continue my studies from the same page, the same line, the same spot where I had left off. Learning saved me."

He goes on. "Maybe that is why I believe so deeply in education. If there is a solution to the problems humanity faces, education must play the central role in it. I know that learning saved me. And I believe it can save us."

Rachel and the other students seem satisfied by this response, but I find myself struggling. I am not as hopeful as our professor. Of course I believe in education, but it is hard for me to see it as a panacea, the solution to the world's problems.

Can learning, as Professor Wiesel claims, really save us? With the myriad seemingly insurmountable challenges we face today, from global warming to the revival of nationalist and populist movements, from hunger and homelessness to religious hatred and fanaticism, is education really the answer?

For most of my life, I have fought to understand the uncomfortable gap between professed values and actual conduct, between lofty aspirations and real-life behavior. When I was a child, learning was a source of joy and comfort to me. My earliest experience of school is still fresh in my mind. I went to a traditional yeshiva, filled with warmth. Many of my teachers were Hasidim who made learning fun. When I was five years old, my classmates and I received our very own *siddurim*, or prayer books, in a special ceremony attended by parents and teachers. I remember standing on a chair, wrapped in a prayer shawl and wearing a crown made of cardboard and glitter, reading a few lines of the morning service. When I was done, my school principal, a rabbi with a black beard and kind eyes, gave me a sugar cube—an ancient tradition meant to symbolize the pleasure of learning. The message was clear and visceral: learning is sweet. To this day I can taste that sugar cube, can feel the pride and pleasure I felt then.

Outside of school I spent every spare moment reading mythology, folktales, and fairy tales and drawing imaginary creatures in pencil and Magic Marker (I loved to draw and knew from an early age that I wanted to be an artist). In my mind, the line between those fantasy worlds and the ancient texts we studied in school began to blur. Both held lessons about how to be a good and noble person, how to deal with challenges, how to complete quests. The teachers spoke gently to their students, wiped away tears when boys skinned their knees, and conferred in whispers about our individual needs. They were refined, decent, and kind; living knights of the spirit.

Though I attended an ultra-Orthodox school, I was not ultra-Orthodox. And my home life was complicated. My parents separated when I was five; when they asked me and my sister what kind of custody arrangement we preferred, we voted to switch homes every day and every weekend. And that is what we did: Monday nights at Dad's, Tuesday nights at Mom's, and so on. We had gotten what we wanted—regular contact with both of them—but the cost of that exchange was a pervasive sense of anxiety and dislocation.

My parents differed in outlook, temperament, and beliefs. My mother, an intellectual who prized learning, insisted I attend an ultra-Orthodox elementary school so that I would gain a strong basis for a thoughtful Jewish life. My father, a composer and free spirit, wanted me to choose public school so that I would have as broad an exposure to modern creative currents as possible. My mother's position won, and I spent my days studying Talmud, with its intricate, often grueling debates, its laws and legends. But I doodled in the margins; spacemen and monsters battled in the narrow columns between texts, starships crossed the abysses between medieval commentators, laser beams blasted through the pages.

At my mother's house, we lived a traditional Orthodox life. During a quiet Friday-night dinner of chicken soup and pot roast with potatoes (my grandmother's recipe), my mother would ask me to share what I had learned in school that week. Later, she and my sister would sing Jewish choral music while I read, then all three of us would read together until we fell asleep. On Shabbat mornings, my mother insisted I attend synagogue, though I sat there alone, a child among septuagenarians. In the afternoon I'd go visit my friends, who lived a long walk away, to play Risk, eat junk food, talk about comic books, and study for upcoming Talmud tests.

At my father's house, observance was looser, and the food —hot dogs, egg rolls, and other takeout—unconventional. On Shabbat my father slept late, waking at two in the afternoon and eating breakfast while my sister and I ate lunch. We enjoyed these informal meals, especially when his friends would come over for extended salon-like sessions, when my father would initiate fascinating discussions about the nature of time and the limits of personal choice ("If a friend wants to commit suicide, do we have the right, or obligation, to stop him?"). My new stepmother would set the timer before Shabbat to video-tape *Dallas*, her favorite show, and we'd hear the click and whir of the machine starting up during the meal. On Saturday after-noons, we'd walk to Riverside Park, and I'd climb on the big rocks, glacial deposits from one and a half million years ago, when New York was covered by a thousand feet of ice.

Sometimes the chasm between the lifestyles in my parents' respective homes led to uncomfortable situations, as when my father was delayed picking me up from a friend's house one Friday afternoon until close to sundown (when, traditionally, Jews cease all work, including driving). My friend's father, an Orthodox Jew, like most of the other parents in my school, asked my father, "How are you going to make it into the city in time for Shabbat?"

My father, perhaps embarrassed, evaded the question, but Mr. Kellerman pressed. "There's no way you can make it in time — you'll have to stay in Queens."

I don't remember how this exchange ended; I only remem-ber my discomfort at my family's being "outed" as less obser-vant than that of my friend. This feeling stayed with me and led to a general sense of living a double life. The demands of observance and the realities of our family could not comfort-ably coexist.

And then there was my sister: blind from birth, sensitive, extremely musical. We shared a room, and when I was little I got angry because she was able to read her Braille books in the dark while mine became indecipherable with the lights out. When we were young we played together, but as we got older I spent more time with my friends, hanging out at the kosher pizza place or comic-book shop. She took my parents' divorce harder than I did, or at least she expressed her feelings about it while I pretended everything was fine.

When we went out to restaurants, I noticed kids from the neighborhood looking at her and whispering. I wanted to shield her, protect her. Having a sibling with special needs made me keenly alert to social dynamics. I noticed outsiders everywhere, in every room, at every birthday party, and I wanted to help them. But how was I supposed to do that when I often felt like an outsider myself?

When I graduated from elementary school, my parents again pulled me in two different directions. My mother supported my attending another black-hat yeshiva, an affiliate of my previous school, while my father again suggested that public school might be a more liberating option. I decided to split the difference and enroll in a Modern Orthodox school. (Modern Orthodoxy developed among German Jews in the mid- to late nineteenth century as a way of harmonizing traditional Judaism with contemporary life and new scientific and historical developments. Its schools offered traditional classes in the mornings and secular subjects in the afternoons.) The days were long. School got out at 6:20, and during the winter months I'd exit the building and be surprised at the dark world outside.

Inside the school, it was sometimes dark too. During the first few weeks in this new high school, I saw the rabbi who had welcomed students at the assembly suddenly grab a kid in the hallway, hold him against the wall by his neck, and yell at him for some infraction. Recess was filled with playground roughhousing as well as serious fights that had to be broken up by teachers. I felt disoriented, like a baby emerging from the womb into a cold place.

The traditional texts were the same ones we studied in my first school, but the connections between text and life seemed frayed. Judging by how my fellow classmates treated one another, many of them clearly hadn't internalized the teachings, and no one corrected the students' behavior. Again and again, we were tested on intricate laws, the details of which seemed to be more important than their underlying purpose. The ethical messages in the text were lost. Conformity was a central cultural value, and kids who were different, including artsy kids like me, were persecuted. I saw a few older kids force a particularly small freshman into a locker, then lean against it while they chatted. Kids competed for grades and often cheated on tests.

The holy books we studied painted a picture of a community where each person's uniqueness was supported and celebrated. But that community didn't actually exist here. When I dared ask about the clear distance between our heritage and our lived values, the rabbis replied that I needed to study a lot more before asking such questions. I flirted with the thought that my religion was morally bankrupt, nothing more than a pose. But, although many of my classmates eventually left religion behind, something held me back. Maybe it was the beauty of my grandparents' Shabbat table, maybe it was my elementary-school teachers, but I had experienced the gifts of the religious world and was reluctant to give up on it.

I was in a state of constant questioning. In my naiveté, I wondered: How could such rich teachings fail to transform people into agents of goodness? Was it possible for a spiritual community to nurture individuality rather than conformity? What would it take for human beings to stop staring and whispering at those, like my sister, who were different?

As a teenager, I looked around at the adults in my life, my parents and teachers, and it seemed to me that they'd all made a choice to privilege either tradition or creativity, dedication to the past or commitment to an idiosyncratic personal vision. I saw no one who fully embodied the bridge I sought between community and self-expression, religion and art.

That November, my mother's future husband, Mati, suggested I go with him to a public lecture by Elie Wiesel, whom he knew through his work as a choral conductor, and I enthusiastically agreed. When he offered to introduce me after the lecture, I *nervously* agreed. I had read several of Wiesel's books and had heard him speak at my high school about the Holocaust. I perceived him as Jewish royalty, and I was in awe.

In my memory, his actual talk was eclipsed by our brief handshake afterward. What I do remember is the small reception room after the public lecture.

IT IS VERY CROWDED. There is a hum and buzz of excitement that swells as the lecturer enters the room. Elie Wiesel is slight, with narrow shoulders, wearing a charcoal-gray suit jacket. On his left lapel is a tiny red and gold French Legion of Honor pin. He walks as if bearing a great weight with grace. Every once in a while, he palms his wispy, wild hair away from his forehead like a cool teenager. His skin is weathered, his face furrowed by deep creases. It looks like a map of the world, if the world had been wounded but still managed to laugh.

A messy line forms, and Mati beckons me forward. A space; here he is. Wiesel holds his hand out to me and says in a clear, light voice with a slight accent, "Elie Wiesel."

I am tongue-tied. This is the man who survived horror to become a confidant of kings and prime ministers. This is the man who traveled to conflict zones so he could bear witness to suffering and who was awarded the Nobel Peace Prize for doing so.

It was only years later that I thought about who and where I was at age fifteen and who and where he was at the same age. The distance between my comfortable American upbringing and his experience of what he often called "the kingdom of night," between my New World and his prewar Judaism, between my native English and his native Yiddish, between the 1980s cartoons that animated my thoughts and the ascetic practices that tempted young Elie—all seemed unbridgeable. And yet somehow, even in that brief moment, I felt, for the first time, fully seen.

The Betrayal of Knowledge

AS TIME WENT ON and I began to read more of Elie Wiesel's books, I came to learn that my questions about the disconnect between learning and living had a parallel in Wiesel's critique of normative education. He had a passion for learning; it did indeed save him, by breaking his isolation after the war and providing meaning and, even more important, the *quest* for meaning. But the gap between humanity's supposed wisdom and the world he lived in troubled him. Whereas my problem emerged from the modest struggles of a sheltered American Jewish kid, his began as he contemplated the meaning-defying experience of the Holocaust.

He had many painful questions to ask, but perhaps the one that drove him to become a teacher was this: Why didn't learning and knowledge inoculate the German people against hatred? It was, after all, this most "advanced" nation on earth, cultured and urbane, professing humanistic values, that led the efforts to eradicate Wiesel's people. As he later told us in class, "One of the darkest days of my life after the war was when I discovered that many of the killers, high-ranking Nazi officials and front-line murderers alike, had advanced university degrees." Many were students and scholars of Goethe and Kant, those great thinkers who explored the concepts of ethics and morality. We have records of SS officers attending church, playing with their children, treating their pets with tenderness, then going off to do their terrible work. Doctors were involved in appalling medical experiments, their commitment to "do no harm" somehow suspended. How is it that the twentieth century shows us example after example of the radical separation of ethics from knowledge? What do we do with the fact that it is possible to acquire knowledge and use it to harm people? Wiesel said, "I always believed that education was a shield, that to be educated means you cannot do certain things. How come that is not correct?"

In response to these questions, Wiesel sought to create a new kind of learning. If neither grand literary concepts nor august philosophical traditions could provide protection against fanaticism, if religion too was susceptible to corruption (and how

many times in history have congregants, inspired by fiery sermons, left places of worship to commit atrocities in the name
of faith?), then what could safeguard moral clarity? Learning
might have saved Elie Wiesel, but it did not save nations from
madness. There had to be a hidden element, one that could
fulfill education's promise to protect against moral and ethical
corruption. Professor Wiesel's life as a teacher became a quest
for this element that would ensure that knowledge became a
blessing and not a curse, that its accumulation would lead to
compassionate behavior and not its opposite. Like a scientist,
he experimented—in his writing, in his meditations, and especially in the classroom—eventually finding and naming this
new element; he called it memory.

I ATTENDED WIESEL'S PUBLIC lectures occasionally in the
months that followed our first meeting. In those early days, I
was too shy to approach him, but I hung on his words, looking for connections between his spoken messages and his writings. I was struck by the way he drew on Jewish teachings to
underscore universal ethical concepts, something the teachers
at my high school certainly didn't do. He was concerned with
the weak and vulnerable, the outsiders and the endangered, in
life and in literature. Human rights, freedom of speech and religion, the plight of the oppressed and of refugees—all were
at the center of his attention. And it was the biblical stories,
the tales from the Talmud that I studied in school, that, in his
world, illuminated the way forward. Suddenly those texts I was
studying for hours every day did not seem irrelevant. Suddenly
my tradition seemed more worthy of my regard. Suddenly the
call of the prophets, the ethical messages within Jewish law,

were urgent and valuable. I sat up a little straighter in class, spent extra hours rereading the texts, and saw a glimmer of possibility for a new path.

And it was not only the ethical message to which Wiesel was awakening me. It was also the stories themselves, the legends, the fables found in the heart of Judaism. Choni the Circle-Maker, Bar Kochba the warrior, the Baal Shem Tov, the scholarly Maiden of Ludmir, began to occupy my imagination, as Gandalf the Grey and Yoda had before. I was thirsty for these stories. Slowly, over months, I began to see that the wildness and mystery that drew me to myths and folktales also existed in my own tradition. And it seemed to me that Elie Wiesel held the keys to this legacy. I began painting scenes from Jewish legend using the same Magic Markers and imagery I had used to portray scenes from Greek myths and comic books. In my paintings, scholars held long swords or shot rays of light from their eyes.

Over the next few years, I read every collection of Jewish tales I could find, in Hebrew and in English, from my grandparents' book collections and from the school library. Some of these collections were old and fusty, with archaic language and heavy-handed moralizing. I preferred the ones that were more open-ended, magical, even surreal: The rabbinic tale of the failed world God created before our own, with its two-headed, four-armed humans whose trouble was that the two heads could never get along. The legends of the Nephilim, the fallen angels who married human women and begot generations of giants and wizards. The mystical tales of Rebbe Nachman (1772–1810), with their seekers, dark forests, and magical castles. In these stories, jungles were overcome with laughter,

animals composed songs to the moon, and children were occasionally made of precious stones. The more I read, the more
I saw how much there was to read—layer upon layer of tale
and commentary, super-commentary, and controversy, a loud,
lively conversation across thousands of years and many continents.

Like most Orthodox Jewish kids, I had an awareness of
the Holocaust. It was taught in school as early as third grade,
though not always as thoughtfully as you might expect. In fifth
or sixth grade, we were shown a video that included images
of bodies in mass graves discovered by Allied troops after the
war. It was like science fiction, one of the late-night shows kids
weren't supposed to watch. I didn't understand why our teachers decided that this was okay for us. I don't remember even
speaking about this moment with friends in school. Looking
back, I think we were dissociating from what we had seen.

At fifteen, I knew that Elie Wiesel had survived the camps.
I had read *Night* and had a sense that he was known as an important spokesperson for survivors. Others who survived also
came and spoke at our school or at local synagogues on Holocaust Remembrance Day, telling their stories, talking about
their lost families. Sometimes they cried.

I was interested in all this, but my friends and I were also re-
pelled. It was scary, too much; we didn't know how to hold the
stories we were being told. We also didn't accept the implicit
message our teachers conveyed that the Holocaust somehow
defined our Jewish lives. We understood that it was a crucial
event but felt that our religion had to have a more positive and
sovereign meaning, that we could not rely on our enemies to
tell us who we were.

One evening a few months after my first meeting with the professor, I was mulling over the day's events, which included a talk by a survivor, and I thought of Wiesel. I began to wonder if he could help me make sense of my confusion, especially the ambivalence I felt about studying the Holocaust. I noticed that much of his writing was about Jewish tales and legends and that his lectures were often framed as a celebration of Jewish history and heroes. He had clearly found a way to honor his experiences without letting them eclipse his connection to our shared tradition. He had lived through the Holocaust but his life's work didn't end there. Most of his writing dealt with other subjects: examinations of literature, contemporary struggles for human rights and dignity, and Jewish legends and personalities. The Holocaust was not his subject; it was the lens through which he looked at all subjects. It was a lens that, I would later learn, he offered his students as well, one that helped us see the connections between literature and history, great books and our personal stories. He taught us to always seek the moral meaning of the texts we read.

FAST-FORWARD TO AUTUMN of 2004, fourteen years after that first meeting. I am now Professor Wiesel's teaching assistant at Boston University, and this is the first meeting of a course titled Faith and Heresy. I am always nervous at the beginning of the semester. I feel like a second-grader on his first day of school, wondering if he forgot his lunchbox, whether he will be able to find his classroom. Students are nervous too on their first day with the famous professor, each of them surrounded by more than sixty other students, most of whom are strangers. They are intimidated by one another, everyone locked up in his or her own projections. I am eager for them to experience the adventure before them.

As usual, Professor Wiesel has asked me to prepare a one-page text to kick off our discussion of the course topic. For Faith and Heresy, I choose a short story by the Hasidic master Rebbe Nachman called "The Tainted Grain" for a few student volunteers to read out loud.

> Once an astrologer-king saw in the stars that anyone who would eat of the coming harvest would go mad. He called in his viceroy and friend to ask for his advice.
>
> "Sire," replied the counselor, "you and I shall eat only last year's harvest, which is untainted. And so we shall remain sane."
>
> But the king replied, "I do not accept your proposal. How can we separate ourselves from our people? To remain the only sane people among a nation of madmen—they will think we are the ones who are mad. Instead, you and I shall eat of the tainted grain, and shall enter into madness with our people."
>
> The king thought for a moment, then said, "We must, however, at least recognize our malady. Therefore, you and I shall mark each other's foreheads with a sign. And every time we look at one another, we shall remember that we are mad."

Professor Wiesel looks around at his students and says, "I envy you. You are just beginning. Or beginning again. So: What do we make of this story?" There is a long moment of silence, which is typical for the very first classroom moments, and the silence expands to fill the high-ceilinged room. But he is comfortable with silence; he waits, and after several seconds, two students raise their hands, and Professor Wiesel nods at the first.

A young woman with large, bright red glasses says, "If the world is mad—"

"Please say your name," interrupts Professor Wiesel.

"Oh, I'm Karen, and I'm from Chicago," she says, only slightly flustered. "If the world is mad, with whatever kind of madness, bad behavior, or just distorted ways of looking at things, then leaders have to stay close to the people to have a chance of helping."

"Good. I need more," says Professor Wiesel, and he looks to the next student whose hand is raised.

"I think—um, I'm Steven and I'm from Allston, I'm studying medicine—I think the king should've stayed sane so that he could help his people. How can you help heal others if you're infected too? This happens with doctors and nurses during epidemics; if they are exposed, then they're *finished,* and that doesn't benefit anyone."

"I'm curious," says a grad student who introduces herself as Marjorie. "What did the author have in mind when he talked about the harvest? What kind of madness was he seeing in the world around him?"

"Well," Professor Wiesel says, "we know that Rebbe Nachman was one of the Hasidic masters who anticipated modernity, and he was afraid of what it would do to the world. He, unlike other masters, spent time with modernizers in the Jewish community and knew them well, discussed philosophy and even played chess with them!

"Therefore it is likely that he knew at least some of what was coming: industrial revolution, mass movements . . . Did he know *more?* Did he anticipate the events that would shape the world in my lifetime? We cannot know. But it is clear that he saw a madness descending on the world, and he was afraid. The world did go mad in the twentieth century. Is the sign that can prevent madness's ultimate victory . . . memory?"

Solé, an African theology student, introduces herself and says, "I have seen this kind of thing before, when real madness sweeps a nation, and the leaders hide behind their fortified walls. They refuse to come out; they do not take responsibility, and people are hurt. But when the leaders go with the people, sometimes things have changed."

I see Professor Wiesel's gaze sharpen.

"Where are you from?" he asks.

Solé says, "I am from Zimbabwe."

"Then you understand this story," he says. "And you must share *your* story."

Later, Solé comes to talk to me during office hours. She explains haltingly that her brother was killed by the Mugabe regime during a protest. She tells me that many of her family members and childhood friends are HIV positive and struggle to find medical care or do without. Indeed, by the early 2000s, unemployment, disease (particularly cholera and HIV), and food shortages were endemic in Zimbabwe, leading to widespread protests against the government of Robert Mugabe, which had been in power for decades. His supporters reacted with intimidation and sometimes extreme violence against their opponents; one of their victims was Solé's brother.

"I'm so sorry. I can't imagine that," I tell her. Then, after a moment: "You know that Professor Wiesel meets with every student in this class, but he will especially want to speak with you. I can help you make an appointment with him for next week if you'd like."

She agrees, and I see her smile for the first time.

Later she told me she met with him for almost an hour. Solé discussed her experiences with him, he asked questions, and they sat in silence for several minutes. At the end, as Solé stood in the open doorway about to leave, Professor Wiesel took her hand gently and said, "I told you in class that you must tell your story. This is because, if even one person learns from it how to be more human, you will have made your memories into a blessing. We must turn our suffering into a bridge so that others might suffer less."

"Write Everything Down": The Shield of Memory

IT WAS TYPICAL OF Professor Wiesel to zero in on a student's history. He was always sensitive to the presence of trauma and cared more about personal consequences than abstract ideas. As a member of a generation haunted by ghosts, Wiesel was on a quest to make his memories redemptive. In a classroom lecture on the topic of memory in modern literature, Professor Wiesel became suddenly personal: "The challenge of our generation of survivors was, *what would we do with our memories?* Would we allow them to drown us in despair, or would they somehow give us the strength to respond to other people's suffering?"

It makes sense that he would interpret the sign on the king's forehead and that of his friend as referring to memory. What else could possibly help us recognize our own madness? What else could help us question the consensus of our peers when they are losing touch with reality? The distinction between an education that can save us and one that can exist comfortably alongside moral compromise, corruption, and evil rests on memory.

But what did he mean by *memory*?

In 1939, at a speech given to Wehrmacht commanders one week before Germany's invasion of Poland, Adolf Hitler is reported to have said, "Who remembers the Armenians?" He was referring to the Armenian genocide, which began in 1915 and is considered by many historians to be the first modern genocide—that is, the first systematic project to destroy a minority population. Hitler's cynical remark was meant to reassure his co-conspirators that their horrific actions would not be censured, that the world would not protest a new genocide. Moral amnesia as invitation to murder.

Professor Wiesel often quoted a Hasidic saying: "Forgetfulness leads to exile, memory to redemption." Time and again, he reminded his classes that memory is our only protection. "My goal is always the same: to invoke the past as a shield for the future." He often referenced the great Jewish historian Shimon Dubnov, who, when facing imminent death in the Riga ghetto, called out to his people: "Jews, write everything down!" Wiesel frequently pointed to the Jewish victims of the Holocaust who, hiding in bunkers from the Nazis, scratched their names into the walls and wrote invisible messages in urine, who buried manuscripts in tin cans under the ghetto streets so that one day their names, their words, their lives might be remembered. He believed that those who lived before us call to us to remember them and that by examining the past, we can create a new future. As Wiesel stated in his Nobel acceptance speech, "If anything can, it is memory that will save humanity."

IN 2013, RHONDA FINK-WHITMAN, an author and daughter of a Holocaust survivor, traveled to Ivy League universities asking students basic questions about the Holocaust. Their answers are striking not just for their ignorance but for the farfetched guesses students offered when pressed. Asked when the Holocaust happened, students' responses included the year 1800. When asked how many Jews were murdered, one student guessed three million, then revised his answer to three hundred million. But this is just one example of a phenomenon that extends far beyond the Holocaust. The specifics of other moral-ground-zero events — the Cambodian genocide in the 1970s, the 1992 breakup of Yugoslavia and the ethnic cleansing that followed, the 1994 genocide in Rwanda, and too many other massacres, genocides, and conflicts — have also been forgotten.

"How can we stop forgetting?" I ask Professor Wiesel one afternoon in his office. I am referring specifically to a recently published FBI report about white supremacist groups and Holocaust denial in the United States.

He sighs as if he knows there is no good answer. But then he says: "History is a narrow bridge. We are naturally afraid of our memories, of the trauma of our memories. We try to forget, and in truth, some things we must forget a little bit, simply in order to function. And yet . . . if we truly allow ourselves to forget, history may well return to us."

After a moment he adds, "You know that this is the reason I teach. And why you will teach too."

The Need for Mirrors

IT IS A CLICHÉ that ignoring history can lead to its repetition. But we also know that the purely technical transmission of information has never been enough to prevent the next tragedy. If memory is to make a moral difference, we need to locate ourselves within it.

In class, Professor Wiesel tells his students another story, one of his favorites from the Hasidic tradition. He smiles as he begins, but his smile fades as the story progresses.

> Once there was a man who was so forgetful that, when he awoke in the morning, he didn't know what to do with the strange objects he found in his room. Every morning saw him painstakingly trying to determine what each item of clothing was for, looking them up in research books, and finally putting them on correctly. This took him hours, and he was always late for work.
>
> One day he decided to label everything in his house. He did so, and the next morning, when he awoke, he looked around. Following the labels' instructions, he dressed—quickly. He recognized a chair from its note and sat on it —quickly. He saw the note on his socks and put them on —quickly.
>
> Then, as he was leaving, his eye fell on the mirror by the door. He looked in the mirror and froze. Bewildered, he whispered, "But who am I?"

"It is not enough to know the facts," Professor Wiesel reminds his students. "We must take things—history, current
events—personally. We must look in mirrors. And great literature can act as a mirror."

Great books, like mirrors, can serve as tools of self-awareness. Through literature, we learn about ourselves, our psychological and ethical natures. In a class on *The Diary of Anne
Frank,* a book that most students had read in middle school,
Professor Wiesel opens his lecture by saying, "Although we
usually think of ourselves as questioners of the text, today
the text will question us." He means that the students must
pay careful attention to their reactions and responses to literature, to the questions to which they return, to the characters that capture their imaginations. In this way, *the books read
them,* shedding light on their leanings and assumptions, raising
self-awareness. Over the course of a semester, students learn
to identify dissonances between text and morality, the places
where we cannot accept the behavior of characters or their authors. Students strive to understand Dostoyevsky's Grand In-
quisitor, Arthur Koestler's corruptly ideological Soviet tribunal
in *Darkness at Noon,* Kafka's faceless judges in *The Trial.* They
also wrestle with their own responsibilities as they study the
events of Cambodia between 1975 and 1979, Rwanda in 1994,
and Darfur in the early 2000s.

Wrestling with Text and Morality

PROFESSOR WIESEL MODELED this kind of wrestling in each class meeting by consistently and sometimes defiantly reading literature through an ethical lens. His readings differed from the usual academic lectures students heard in other class-rooms. He expressed sympathy for those characters whose au-thors made them suffer so much, and this sympathy guided his interpretations. Often, he would tell us he loved a particular character, and then he'd smile and explain why. At first I was surprised by this. I was used to professors who emphasized au-thors' intentions and agendas, the historical context in which a work was created, the positions and beliefs for and against which it was arguing. I might sympathize with a character, but so what? Why should that matter? In my other college classes, the teachers' likes and dislikes and what the students found res-onant or dissonant were unimportant.

A student named Gina helped me grasp what our teacher was doing. "I feel a little embarrassed by this," she told me one day after class, "but I think Professor Wiesel is nicer to fictional characters than I am to real people. Now I'm trying to be a lit-tle kinder to my family and friends." Gina was beginning to see that reading literature and reading life were deeply entangled actions. So was I.

In a discussion of violence in the Hebrew Bible, Professor Wiesel pointed out that the biblical book of Joshua, which con-tains the story of the Israelites conquering Canaan and put-ting many of its inhabitants to the sword, includes no songs, no poetry; he commented, "Where there is violence, there can be no poetry." Even sacred texts must not be immune to ethical criticism.

In this, he was following in the footsteps of Jewish tradition, which values wrestling with text, with others, even with God (the Hebrew word *Israel* literally means "he who wrestles with God"). In his syllabus choices, he emphasized archetypal moral situations. In a lecture on a novel about Kosovo, he offered his students this rule of thumb: "Whatever you learn, remember: the learning must make you more, not less, human."

ONE DAY IN THE Faith and Heresy class, I see a student named Nadia raise her hand and then lower it several times. Born and raised in Germany, a granddaughter of a former SS officer, she has enrolled in this course bearing a heavy load of family history. In class, she is extremely shy and has not yet spoken up, but now she clearly has a burning question to ask. I catch her eye and nod encouragingly. *Go ahead,* I think. She raises her hand and this time she keeps it up. Professor Wiesel smiles and calls on her.

"Can any good result from evil, and can evil result from good?" In our discussion section earlier that day we talked about the forced medical experiments that took place in concentration camps, some of which led to medical breakthroughs. Students were divided as to whether it was moral to benefit from these experiments. I know that she is also thinking of her grandfather.

Professor Wiesel begins to answer her question, quoting sources both ancient and modern about the unintentional beneficence of the wicked and the redemption of evil. Then, suddenly, in a tone that is nonnegotiable, almost fierce, he says,

"But the key in all of this is: Never allow anyone to be humiliated in your presence. Whatever has happened in the past, we must deal with those who are here *now.*"

Months later, Nadia tells me that this concise statement of humanism was the foundation on which she began building a response to the shadow cast by her grandfather's role.

If Professor Wiesel read literature through an ethical lens, he read history through a literary lens, a subscriber to the Hasidic teaching that the world and the text are commentaries on each other.

In a lecture on *The Dybbuk,* a Yiddish play written in the early 1900s about a young woman possessed by a demon, Professor Wiesel makes a connection to modern fanaticism.

"Is it possible that the demonic can possess not only individuals, but nations?" he asks his students. "Is this what happened in my lifetime to the German people and others?"

Erica, a creative writing student with thick glasses, counters with another question. "Was the demon really exorcised from Germany after 1945, given the new wave of anti-Semitism?"

"It was, to a large extent," Professor Wiesel says. "And it was the young people who did that work. It's true, there are far-right fanatics again in Germany. But there are also many young people fighting against fanaticism. Ultimately, I trust the young people. They give me hope."

After class, Nadia knocks on my office door. She is clearly upset.

"Why did Professor Wiesel say that about the demon possessing the German people, my people?" she begins. My immediate thought is *She is upset because he implied criticism of her entire nation.* But she goes on.

"Why did he describe what happened as possession? This takes away responsibility from the Germans. They *were* responsible. They made choices, terrible choices; they were not being forced by some otherworldly power!"

"It's a good question," I respond cautiously, "and I wonder what he meant. Let's look at the text we were discussing, *The Dybbuk*." I think for a minute. "If I remember correctly, in the play, the demon can't enter a person unless it is invited in. I think that he was not absolving the German people of their responsibility—after all, they invited the demon in. But once the demon enters, it can go far beyond any original intention."

We turn the pages together, looking for the moment of the demon's first appearance. We find it: a pleading call from the protagonist, the young woman, to her dead beloved—an invitation. Nadia likes this answer, and I encourage her to talk to Professor Wiesel about her questions. I am moved by her sincerity and diligence in wrestling with her nation's legacy. She is not reading with the critical distance of an academician. She is reading as a moral actor.

"I Cannot Sleep Since for What I Have Seen": *Witnessing History in Real Time*

HAVING A TEACHER WHOSE ROLE extended beyond the classroom brought our learning to life. Students frequently asked Professor Wiesel about current world events, especially in the final class of the semester. "What is really happening to the dissidents in Iran?" "Is there truth to what we are hearing in the news about the potential for renewed peace talks in the Middle East?" "Why isn't the U.S. government doing more to intervene in Darfur?" His responses were often informed by conversations with heads of state, foreign ministers, and politically active friends.

When we studied the Rwandan genocide, he shared with the class his frustration at the inaction of the world community and the U.S. government. He told us that, through public speeches and private conversation, he had tried to influence the U.S. administration to intervene on behalf of the Tutsis and stem the tide of murder. He had failed. Although President Clinton later apologized for U.S. inaction—in itself an unprecedented symbolic gesture—the loss of more than eight hundred thousand lives attests to the limits of eloquence. As Professor Wiesel was recounting his attempts to reach world leaders, his grief was palpable. We had spent weeks exploring the themes of oppression, genocide and intervention, and the responsibility of survivors and witnesses to prevent future tragedies. As we listened to our teacher's account of his attempts to effect sustainable moral change, history was no longer an abstraction.

A student named Aaron asked, "Did you ever succeed in convincing a president to change U.S. foreign policy?"

Professor Wiesel paused before replying: "Once." He was referring to his public call to action at the opening of the U.S. Holocaust Memorial Museum in Washington, DC, in April of 1993. It was raining at the event, and the paper Wiesel's speech was written on became soaked and unreadable, so he spoke extemporaneously. At the end of his remarks, he said:

And, Mr. President, I cannot *not* tell you something. I have been in the former Yugoslavia last fall. I cannot sleep since for what I have seen! As a Jew I am saying that we must do something to stop the bloodshed in that country! People fight each other and children die. Why? Something, anything must be done.

President Clinton later said that Wiesel's rebuke was a key reason for his decision to begin supporting peacekeeping efforts in Yugoslavia. "He said, in his polite way, I needed to get off my rear end and do something about Bosnia."

Professor Wiesel told us that he had not planned to speak about Yugoslavia at that forum. The rain forced him off script, and when he spoke from the heart, this critical message emerged. This taught Wiesel's students an empowering lesson: it is at the intersection of history and humanity, when we leave the script and step into the unknown, that powerful change can take place.

And It Was Enough

ONE DAY IN CLASS, Annika, a third-year communications major, asks, "How can we, students with comfortable lives, really understand your experiences, much less pass them on to others?"

Because memory is the secret ingredient that creates a morally transformative approach to learning, this question is vital. How does one educate toward memory? How can students become custodians of memories that are not their own?

Professor Wiesel smiles slightly and says, "You are correct that this is *the* question. As we know, it is not simply a matter of information. Our task is to awaken sensitivity to others' suffering. And this is not a simple task." He continues with a story:

> When Rebbe Israel Baal Shem Tov, the founder of Hasidism, saw that the Jewish people were threatened by tragedy, he would go to a particular place in the forest where he lit a fire, recited a particular prayer, and the miracle was accomplished, averting the tragedy.
>
> Later, when the Baal Shem Tov's disciple the Maggid of Mezrich had to intervene with heaven for the same reason, he went to the same place in the forest, where he told the Master of the Universe that while he did not know how to light the fire, he could still recite the prayer, and again, the miracle was accomplished.
>
> Later still, Rebbe Moshe Leib of Sasov, in turn a disciple of the Maggid of Mezrich, went into the forest to save his people. "I do not know how to light the fire," he said to God, "and I do not know the prayer, but I can find the place and this must be sufficient." Once again, the miracle was accomplished.
>
> When it was the turn of Rebbe Israel of Rizhyn, the great-grandson of the Maggid of Mezrich who was named after the Baal Shem Tov, to avert the threat, he sat in his armchair, holding his head in his hands, and said to God: "I am unable to light the fire, I do not know the prayer, and I cannot even find the place in the forest. All I can do is tell the story. That must be enough." And it was enough.

Professor Wiesel lets his gaze travel around the room as he says, "Like the rebbe of Rizhyn, we may not know how to light the fire, we may not know the prayer, and we may not know the place in the forest. Our connection to the past is weak; it may be distant, at a remove. All we can do is tell the story, and we must. But in order to *tell* the story, we must first *hear* the story."

At the heart of Elie Wiesel's mission as a teacher was a phrase his students heard him repeat time and again: "Listening to a witness makes you a witness." Like propaganda, its evil twin, moral education is contagious. And to be effective, it *must* be contagious. Unlike propaganda, though, which tells people what they want to hear or feeds their existing fears, moral education tells people what they *need* to hear, even when it is painful. "Here is how you can tell the difference between false prophets and true ones," he explained to the class more than once. "The former comfort, while the latter disturb."

When moral education works, students investigate and embrace new ways of thinking, learn new habits of questioning, and, ultimately, find a deeper sense of common humanity. Students who experience this become sensitized to suffering. They read the news differently. They are no longer able to pass a homeless person on the street without offering at least a smile. They speak up when they overhear a bigoted word or see a bully. Inaction is no longer an option.

In order to transform, moral education must entail more than a transactional exchange of information. It is not only the content of what is taught—the history, the data—but the context that defines impact. It is the emotional relationship between student, teacher, and subject. It is the implicit *Why?* at the heart of learning. People are morally ignited less by the cognitive processing of learning information than by visceral experience, less by the intellect than by the nervous system: moments of gooseflesh, chills up the spine, the welling up of tears. This is why moral education struggles to find a home in typical university settings and even in many religious communities. Yet this is the only way a student can become a witness.

IT IS THE LAST class of 2007, and, as usual, students are invited to ask questions about anything they want: the themes and literature they've studied in the previous months, current events and geopolitical dynamics, even Professor Wiesel's own life. Students are usually shy, but they do ask wide-ranging questions, often ones that have preoccupied them throughout the semester.

On this occasion, after they ask about Iran's nuclear program, various political issues, and the role of students in local and national activism, there is a lull. Into this silence, a student sitting in the front row quietly and diffidently asks, "Can you show us your number?"

I do not know how Professor Wiesel will react. I think of the Holocaust-denial websites I've seen, the ones that make my stomach churn, the ones that claim that he doesn't really have a tattoo, that his story is a fiction. I am amazed at this student's chutzpah, and I see the young man turn bright red, possibly regretting his brazen request.

Without a word, Professor Wiesel removes his jacket, unbuttons his cuff, and rolls his shirtsleeve up. He holds his arm before him defiantly and turns so the entire class can see the number tattooed on his forearm.

A collective gasp seizes the room, followed by a long, extended moment of silence.

If despair is contagious, so is memory: memory of the past, of our values, and even, as Hasidic teaching has it, of the future for which we yearn. And because listening to a witness makes you a witness, in reading these words, you, the reader, have become a witness too.

2

Otherness

It is the otherness of the other that fascinates me.

— ELIE WIESEL

IT'S 1996, AND I AM SITTING in my first lecture as a college sophomore, about to get my first taste of Professor Wiesel's class at Boston University. It's the beginning of the semester, and the course is titled Jewish Women's Voices. Professor Wiesel starts with the biblical story of Adam and Eve.

"From the beginning, Genesis teaches us how to be human together. One of the first things we notice in the story of man and woman is the reason given for Eve's creation. The verse tells us that her mission is to be an *ezer k'negdo*—literally, a helper *against* him. *Ezer* means 'helper,' *k'negdo* means 'against him.' Why *against* him? The rabbinic commentators tell us that this teaches us a model of friendly antagonism, one in which, in order to support you, I challenge you. My intentions are for the sake of our friendship, so that your thinking is clarified, your ideas refined within the bounds of our conversation. The first couple are also the first friends, the first strangers, the first to encounter an other. What does it mean to disagree *for the sake of* the other rather than in order to defeat or silence the other?"

We define ourselves by the stories we tell, and our entrenchment in those stories can lead to conflict, he says. For a time, it was common for human beings to burn other humans at the stake over competing cosmologies. Wars have been caused by disputes over textual interpretation. Our differences—skin color, language, accent, wardrobe—still lead us to murder.

Are we wired for conflict? Is war an essential aspect of human history and society? Or is there another way to engage with the other? To listen to him or her with respect? Is it possible for human beings to live in peace? These are some of the questions with which we will wrestle in this course, Professor Wiesel tells us.

The Search for Home

ONE YEAR EARLIER, I had applied to several universities. When it became clear that I had a choice of two Boston-area colleges, I chose the one where Elie Wiesel was a professor.

As an earnest eighteen-year-old, I wanted to study the history of human beings' search for meaning. But there's no major in Meaning Studies, so I opted for the closest thing I could find: religion. The tension between my parents' respective belief systems had long been a source of anxiety, but it had also spurred my desire to understand my own assumptions. The first class I signed up for was the one my old rabbis would have found the most distasteful: Old Testament 101, a course that examined the Bible from an academic point of view. I'd studied these texts from a religious perspective all my life, and now I wanted to look at them from a new angle, to challenge my own deeply held beliefs by learning about those of others.

Being at college was like being an immigrant in a strange new country. In many ways I was a typical American kid, but in others I was from the Old World of Jewish devotion, study, and faith. My roommate, a theater major, and my neighbors, mostly jocks, were like aliens to me. The loud parties and coed bathrooms were jarring. I felt disoriented and was both drawn to and leery of college life.

After Jewish day school with its dual curriculum (Hebrew studies in the morning, secular subjects after lunch, with the school day ending at 6:20 p.m.), my new academic schedule was a breeze. I had plenty of time on my hands, even with studying and writing papers. I made some friends, and we'd spend evenings discussing books, social justice issues, and our dreams of the future. Yet, although I searched, I didn't find a place, a club, or a student group that fit. I knew that my Old Testament class met in the same building where Professor Wiesel had his office, but I was too intimidated to go see him. Then, in my second month of college, I received a message through my stepfather that the professor was waiting for me to come and say hello.

I made an appointment through Martha, Professor Wiesel's longtime assistant. She was a kind but fierce gatekeeper who ensured that the many students, faculty members, and random denizens of Boston who wanted to see Wiesel did not overwhelm him.

I went to see him a few weeks later. We sat in his book-lined office, and I was distracted by all the large, leather volumes. "So. How are you?" Professor Wiesel asked me with a warm smile.

I told him that things were generally good but that I felt I hadn't yet found my place, not even in the Jewish community on campus, where I felt simultaneously more and less religious than the others. I wanted to disappear into contemplative waters, to pray until I lost myself, to finally let go of self-consciousness. At the same time, I loved Maurice Sendak, the Velvet Underground, Allen Ginsberg. I was yearning for a place where I need leave nothing behind, a community that would welcome my mind and heart. I told Professor Wiesel that I felt more at home in small Hasidic prayer houses, with their unassuming décor and Old World feel, than I did at college. When I'd visited one of these shuls in New York, I sat next to an old man. I saw how he swayed back and forth, heard how he prayed in Hebrew with a pronounced Eastern European accent, and I thought: *What is your story, old Jew?* I wondered how that story would compare to the polished, self-conscious stories we so often wrote nowadays.

"I know what you mean," Professor Wiesel said. He told me that he still chose to pray at the smaller Hasidic places when he could, though his regular synagogue on the Upper East Side was a wealthy and modern institution. We spoke of our love for the cadences of Talmud and the humor of Yiddish, the constant references to old texts and quotes from medieval commentators, the wordless melodies running through conversations. He and I felt the same echoes in our bones, though we came from such different places. I saw him as someone deeply connected to both the Old World and the New, and when he said, "We are here, after all, to build bridges between worlds," this was a relief.

He asked what classes I was taking, and I told him: Old Testament, Intro to Comparative Religion, Art History, and a multiyear great-books course the school called the Core Curriculum. He asked what we were reading for that course, and I told him the *Tao te Ching*.

"Ah, Lao Tzu. Do you agree with him that human beings are born as fully formed moral beings, or do you think Confucius was correct that we are born wild and in need of moral education in order to become human?"

I hesitated, surprised to be asked such a question at our first meeting. I chose Lao Tzu's view, perhaps influenced by my father's sixties music with its message of longing for a return to a pristine state ("We've got to get ourselves back to the garden"). Wiesel listened with grave attention, and I felt a little foolish.

After a silence, I told him I'd love to take one of his classes. He said, "Usually I don't accept freshmen into my class. Why don't you wait until next year?" Perhaps he found my answer to his question shallow. Perhaps it had been.

So I waited. I spent the year reading anthologies of tales from the early years of the Hasidic movement. I was struck by the depth of some of these stories, and I had my favorites. Simcha Bunim, the Polish master, a rebel who dressed in modern clothing and worked as a lumberjack and, later, as a pharmacist, spoke to me deeply. His message was "Be authentic, no matter the cost." I started to see that there existed a Jewish version of the enlightenment spoken of in Eastern spirituality, and I wanted in.

The role of the rebbe (pronounced "*reb*-ee") in Hasidism is difficult to describe. The word *rebbe* is translated variously as "teacher," "saint," and "guru," but the rebbe is something else; he is simultaneously traditional and creative; rooted in Jewish text and practice, yet wild and iconoclastic. In school we had rabbis, men whose primary job was to convey information and acculturate us to the rhythms of religious life and practice. But a rebbe, unlike a rabbi, is more than an authority figure — he is a friend, a guide, a supporter of each student's spiritual journey. Where a rabbi builds community and emphasizes its norms, a rebbe builds souls and nurtures individuality. I began to notice a tiny new feeling in my chest, and after a few weeks I realized what it was: the yearning for a rebbe.

According to Hasidic legend, a rebbe sees your past lives, the "root of your soul," the essence of who you were before you lost your way, and he helps you get back to that essence and the road you are meant to walk. Though Elie Wiesel never claimed to be a rebbe, and I wasn't expecting any mystical experiences, I came to his classroom looking for an intellectual and spiritual home.

"We Are Storytellers Too"

I ENROLLED IN ONE of Professor Wiesel's courses the following year. When I entered the classroom on the first day, I could see that this was different from the other courses I'd taken. It was a large seminar with the feel of a small discussion section. The classroom seemed tiny to me, and I later heard that many other students thought this too, but it was actually quite big. Students filled the seats, sat in the aisles, even perched on the windowsills. In other large seminars, you could doodle during class or even nap unnoticed, provided you didn't snore. But here, everyone's eyes were wide open, and returning students who had taken Professor Wiesel's courses in previous years greeted one another like old friends. Also, unlike any other classes I'd taken, this one was multigenerational. The presence of retirees made it feel a bit like a family gathering.

At the beginning of class, Professor Wiesel said, "In twenty years, I hope you will meet someone from this room and that you will say to one another, 'Didn't we study Kafka together?' 'Didn't we discuss Kierkegaard together?' I hope you will build and celebrate friendships." Later, he said, "Friendship is my religion. And it's a good religion; one can be a fanatic of friendship, but so what? So you will be an extremist? Then you will simply be an excellent friend!"

He also said, "As much as you will learn from me, I will learn from you," and I remember hearing these words and feeling both welcomed and challenged. Later, it occurred to me that this simple statement positioned students as contributors, not merely passive recipients—a key principle for creating an active and participatory learning space. It followed a Talmudic teaching that stated "as much as the calf wants to nurse, the heifer wants to give milk." What would teachers do without their students' questions, their curiosity, even their confusion? Teachers and students need each other; together, they form a living ecosystem.

Professor Wiesel believed that every student, every person,

by virtue of being human, had a voice — a distinctive truth. In a lecture on the Hasidic renaissance, Professor Wiesel told a tale:

> Once a young woman came to the wise man asking for the blessing of a child.
>
> "My husband and I have been married for several years, and we still have an empty home," she said.
>
> "You know," the wise man replied, "my mother had the same problem. And she visited the holy Besht [founder of the Hasidic movement] to ask for his blessing. She brought him a coat that she had sewn with her own hands over many weeks, and when she gave it to him he blessed her with a child. I was born one year later."
>
> "Thank you, Teacher," the woman exclaimed. "I will go home right away and begin sewing a coat for you. It will be beautiful, I will use the best wool and the finest colors, and I will return as soon as possible!"
>
> "My dear," said the wise man, "you do not understand. You see, my mother did not know this story."

"It is not enough to repeat the stories of the past; we must also write new ones," Professor Wiesel explained. "We must step off the page into our own situation, which is unmapped and unknown."

He continued, "And yet, we might ask the wise man of the tale why, if he wanted the young woman to find her own answer, he told her a story at all. Ironically, he used a tale of the past to teach that we must find our own answers, our own expressions, our own truths. Without the old tales, we lose faith in our ability to find good responses to today's challenges. The past is there to remind us that we are storytellers too."

But we did not tell the same stories. The diversity of the students produced tension in classroom discussions. The encounter between the child of a Holocaust survivor and the granddaughter of an SS officer was fruitful *because* of their very different starting points. As long as the ground rules were clear —good listening, respectful dialogue, no personal attacks— students would be "helpers against" one another.

I saw this commitment at work in class when a student named Alex, who was born in Russia, asked a question about the Holocaust. "Wasn't it also Russian citizens who were victims of the Nazis, not just Jews?" This question echoed the official Soviet party line about the Holocaust. Until recently, public memorials to Holocaust victims in the Soviet Union almost never mentioned Jews. This had changed due to the efforts of Wiesel and others, but students of Holocaust history generally found questions like this offensive.

I thought, *Uh-oh.*

But Professor Wiesel didn't blink. He was listening for what Alex had not said, or even realized.

He asked Alex, "Did you learn that somewhere? Where?"

"Yes, in school, growing up in Russia, this is what I heard."

"Did you know that what you describe was the official position of the Soviet Union, which as a matter of policy downplayed specific ethnic or religious identities?"

"No, I didn't. But isn't it true that there were other victims?"

"Of course, not all victims were Jews. But all Jews were victims; they were targeted for being Jews, regardless of nationality, political position, or role in society."

Alex replied with a different, deeper formulation of his original question: "Okay. But if a victim has more than one identity

—say, he is a Jew and a Soviet citizen—which identity should we remember?"

At this point, I was no longer embarrassed for Alex but curious, even impressed. I realized that there was something valuable beneath the surface of Alex's original question.

Professor Wiesel didn't believe there were such things as poor students or stupid questions. He trusted that, beneath the surface, there was always something of value to discover. This exchange took about four minutes, but it felt much longer. How many teachers would have shut down the question and moved on quickly to avoid the awkwardness of the moment, or dismissed Alex as a poor student?

The Soul Is Always Whispering

"IN HIS NOBEL PRIZE acceptance speech, William Faulkner said that the only thing really worth writing about is the human heart in conflict with itself. There is a mirroring that happens between inner and outer hospitality. The more we are able to accept the many aspects of who we are, however contradictory those aspects are, the more easily we can accept others, with all *their* contradictions."

When I heard Professor Wiesel say this in a lecture on Walt Whitman's "Song of Myself" ("Do I contradict myself? / Very well then I contradict myself / I am large, I contain multitudes"), I thought about my own story. As someone with a clamorous inner life who was seeking wholeness and quiet, I felt the challenge of fully accepting the seeming contradictions within me. But I had never seen inner conflict as a driver of the judgments people make about one another. I suddenly understood: the extent to which we accept ourselves is the extent to which we have a chance to truly accept others.

"You, too, are vast; each of you contains multitudes. When you enter this room, leave nothing at the door," Professor Wiesel told the class. "Your stories make this class come alive.

"I am looking," he said, "for the essence of each of you to emerge here, so that, together, we can learn what we do not allow ourselves to learn elsewhere." Then he shared with us a conversation recorded in a Hasidic book between a teacher and his disciple:

> "The soul is always whispering to us," taught Rabbi Pinchas of Koretz.
> "Then why don't we change?" asked his disciple Reb Raphael of Bershad.
> "Because," said Reb Pinchas, "the soul never repeats itself."

"Each of us has an indivisible, an ineffable self," Professor Wiesel added. "To encroach upon this essence is a moral offense."

IN THE MIDDLE OF the first semester of my sophomore year, it was finally my turn to give the ten-minute presentation for Professor Wiesel's class. When I signed up on the first day, I had not anticipated how nervous I'd be. I was to discuss the early Hasidic masters, and I hoped to provide some context based on the work of philosopher Martin Buber and some other reading I'd done. I was excited to present on a subject with which I was falling in love, but I was overcome by anxiety. The night before the presentation I hardly slept, going over my notes again and again, hoping I could speak without a tremor in my voice. When I arrived at the classroom, Martha stood at the front where Wiesel usually stood and announced that this was the one class of the semester that our professor had to miss — he was in Paris for a conference, and the TAs would be running today's class. Relieved and disappointed, I gave my presentation.

In class I was usually extremely shy. I sat in the back of the room, attentive but quiet, letting Professor Wiesel's voice and words lull me into a contemplative, relaxed state. I had said one word the entire semester, and that was only when he asked a question and looked at me pointedly. I've forgotten the question, but I will never forget the answer. I realized he was waiting, so I spoke out loud the word that I had been thinking. The word was *authenticity*.

He nodded at me and said, "Exactly."

Sometimes a single word is the key to a new universe. At the semester's end, I was approached by Martha, who told me that Professor Wiesel wanted me to consider becoming his teaching fellow the following year.

I still don't really know why he invited me to play this role. Looking back, I see a kid, sincere, with a seriousness that might have resonated with the man who was to become my mentor, but directionless and pretty immature. Maybe he identified with my shyness or my background in traditional Jewish study. For a long time, I wondered if he had made some kind of mistake. But it was an academic question, because I turned down his invitation.

I had already decided to study in Israel for a year. Before I started college, my teachers had pushed me to do this — kids from my Orthodox high school typically took a gap year in a yeshiva (a traditional academy for advanced text study) before starting college. I went to college first because I wanted to expand my horizons, to begin again outside the narrow confines of the community in which I'd grown up. After two years of college, though, I felt I owed myself time to dive into the sacred texts, my mind bolstered now by at least some experience of modern scholarship.

So when Professor Wiesel invited me to be his teaching assistant, I felt conflicted. I shared my dilemma with him, telling him that I was honored by his invitation but that I also felt a strong pull to Israel and traditional study.

Then I thought of an outside-the-box solution. I naively asked Professor Wiesel if he would consider granting me rabbinic ordination, my idea being that I would study with him over several years toward that degree. This way, I'd be able to study with him while also focusing my time on religious rather than academic subjects. Maybe I could even study with him over the phone from Israel.

"I can't," he said. "I don't have ordination myself!" He told me that a teacher of his, Saul Lieberman, had wanted Elie to become a rabbi, but he had refused, feeling that his was a writer's and not a clergyman's path. (He quoted an old Jewish joke, a play on words in Hebrew. In the High Holidays service, we say, *"V'salachta l'avonenu ki rav hu,"* which means, "Forgive our transgressions, for they are many." The word meaning "many," *rav,* can also be translated as "rabbi," rendering the verse "Forgive us our transgressions — it's the rabbi's fault!")

Finally, reluctant to turn down his TA invitation in person, I sent him a long letter. I wrote, *I am ambitious; I want both worlds. I want the academy and the yeshiva, the breadth of comparing traditions, and the depth of diving into my own.* The next day I called him.

He told me that he had read my letter, that he understood my decision.

I asked him: "In the meantime, is there a way for me to learn with you?"

He said, "Israel is far. But I will let you know when I come there, and we can meet."

Then he said, "I will wait for you. When you are ready, come back and you will study with me."

Was he being polite? Avoiding awkwardness? Was this some sort of commitment? I would find out only several years later.

The Otherness of the Other

THOSE YEARS PASSED. It is 2003. Now, as Professor Wiesel's teaching assistant, I have the responsibility for creating a draft syllabus for each course. I bring this draft to Professor Wiesel, who takes it with him to his New York home to edit; he adds a book, removes another, and sends back a note asking me to include supplementary articles. Though he offers different courses each year, avoiding repetition, certain themes recur. One of these is the theme of difference, diversity, otherness.

If we pay attention to the ways we discuss difference and diversity in our culture, we will notice hidden biases and leanings. In New England, where I live now, we often celebrate connection, speaking of what unites us as being greater than our differences. This is good, but it can lead to a subtle tyranny of sameness, to people living in echo chambers in which they surround themselves with those who think like them. Social media often exacerbates the problem.

In order to fight this tendency, Professor Wiesel emphasized difference. "It is the otherness of the other that fascinates me . . . What can I learn from him? What does he see that I do not, cannot?" In his writing and teaching, he celebrated the madmen, the rebels, the outsiders, the underdogs—the others in literature and in life.

We each have blind spots, just as every candle casts its own shadow. Only when you place a second candle next to the first do the shadows disappear, illuminated by the other's light. The beginning of dialogue is the knowledge that we can do this for one another.

HERE IS PROFESSOR WIESEL lecturing on Kafka, the master artist of alienation: "Kafka wrote, 'I am a cage in search of a bird.' What did he mean? That he recognized his own natural human desire to impose upon, to define, the other. Yet we remember what Kierkegaard wrote: 'Once you label me you negate me.' Kafka wrote *The Trial* and other works to remind us that we must not give in to the impulse to cage others; we must instead guard the otherness of the other."

Tammy, who grew up in the southern United States and has talked before about the endemic racism in her family, asks, "But how can we tolerate someone whose beliefs are fundamentally opposed to ours?"

Professor Wiesel says, "I don't like the word *tolerate*. Who am I to tolerate you? I prefer the word *respect*. I must respect you even if I do not agree with you. In fact, my disagreement may be an expression of my respect for you. If I truly respect you, don't I owe you my honesty?"

"What about truly evil people?" Tammy asks.

"For my own sake, I must still acknowledge their humanity. To act as if the perpetrator of evil is not human is to excuse him too easily. Animals do not commit mass murder. Not only that; animals do not make promises. We must remember to believe the enemy's promises, for whatever he says, he will eventually do. If you think of him as simply an animal or a madman, it will be too easy to dismiss his words. The killer is as human as we are, but he has chosen to betray his humanity. Therefore, I must oppose him, stop him where I can, protest where I cannot."

Tammy is not satisfied. Are her racist uncles "other"? Or are they merely the products of their education, misguided but still worthy of her affection?

"You know," says Professor Wiesel, "for many years I was a journalist, and I was one of those who covered the Eichmann trial in Jerusalem. This was in 1961, after Eichmann was captured in Argentina by the Israelis. I had seen him once, in my little town in May 1944, though I did not know at the time who he was. He came with fifty Hungarian soldiers, and they deported the fifteen thousand Jews of my town. I only learned this later. And so I went to the trial to see whether he was human. Did he have two eyes, two ears; could he speak, smile? To murder so much must leave a mark on a man. At the trial, I watched him, day after day, hoping somehow that I would discover his inhumanity, that I would see some sign that he was *not* human, a mark of Cain. It would have been a great relief to see such a sign. But I saw nothing but a man, a bureaucrat, an accountant. Which means that two human beings made of the same elements, living in the same moment, the same place, may inhabit different moral universes."

He continues: "In fact, Eichmann had a son who did not know his father's blood-soaked past. When he found out, he still expressed love and respect for his father. Another son of a killer became a Catholic priest in an attempt to atone for his father's unatonable sins. What does all this mean? It means that the most inhuman person is still human and will be judged accordingly. The ultimate other is a human being who has renounced his humanity, and we must bring him to justice. But this is the ultimate, the extreme. In our lives, most of the time we encounter simply the other, someone with vastly different beliefs. And we must struggle to understand him, to learn from him. The distance between us is necessary, not something to turn away from."

Geoff asks, "Can you give an example of what this looks like in daily life?"

Professor Wiesel says, "I hope that you encounter the other here, in this room, those who hold different beliefs, values, worldviews than you do. When you do, you are faced with a choice. The choice is to listen, or not. I hope that you listen, really listen, not to find the other's weakness but to find his strength. To disagree, to engage with controversy, does not mean to refuse to listen. On the other hand, to agree with someone does not mean to merge with the other. We are different; we have our own histories, our own destinies."

"But," says Tammy, "if I disagree strongly, don't I have an obligation to try to convince the other person he or she is wrong?"

"That is fine, but the question is, how do you do that? Hegel said that real tragedies are not conflicts between right and wrong; they are conflicts between two rights. And there is a wonderful Hasidic teaching about this that says when two people disagree, and each one pulls away to his own side, his own opinion, a space is created between them. In this space, worlds can be created, provided the two antagonists do not fill the space with too many words. It is only because two people disagree that there can be such a space; were they to hold identical positions, there would be no room for innovation. In other words, conflict can be a good thing—if it is done well."

"But why not try to identify with everyone, find what unites us?"

"Of course we must find what unites us," says Professor Wiesel. "But we must not allow that search to collapse the distinctions between us. We know that in the Middle Ages, Church inquisitors tortured and burned people for the good of their victims' souls. From the accounts that we have, we know that this sentiment was heartfelt, sincere. Therefore, we see that compassion itself is not enough; it is actually dangerous when it is married to the collapse of the otherness of the other. If I believe the other is identical to me, then I may apply my own calculus of pain and salvation to him. If, however, I acknowledge that his values, his priorities, are different, and if I respect that difference, then I can avoid this temptation.

"For the believer, there is a theological element to this as well. I must respect your otherness because it emerges from the ultimate other, God. Each of us is alone as God is alone. So who am I to judge you? I am a witness, not a judge. You know, in the *Inferno* of Dante, God is never referred to by name; the word *God* does not appear. Instead, the word *Other* is used. And this is true also in the book of Esther—God's name does not appear. But these two elisions are for very different reasons. In the *Inferno*, because the characters are in hell, it is forbidden to speak God's name. In Esther, it is because this book explores God's hiddenness in history, how God works through natural or political processes. But in both places, God is the other. Once we really know that we are strangers to one another, we can begin to truly respect one another. From this respect, friendship can develop."

Rather than collapse the distance between us, between our worldviews and opinions, we need to sustain the gap, he says. In this way, we serve as "helpers against," friendly antagonists, partners in clarifying our thoughts. Many of us spend so much moral energy on promoting connection that we sometimes forget to truly celebrate difference. We profess that all human beings are familiar to us. We claim to be so comfortable with different people, religions, ethnic groups, languages, skin colors, face shapes, that we no longer see them. There is a certain kind of jadedness that comes with such tolerance. Nothing surprises us anymore, and it is difficult to respect what you do not see.

Despite following a long line of mystics, Wiesel taught the very opposite approach. Rather than seeing the other as familiar, see the familiar as other, as if you haven't seen that person before. He once told me that the highest level of friendship is when you never entirely know each other but instead always

see each other anew, with a sense of surprise and an inability
to take the other for granted.

"We Are Here to Learn Together": Interreligious Dialogue

JUST AS HE HELPED us see one another with fresh eyes, Professor Wiesel helped us see familiar literature anew. For students who grew up reading Genesis in church or synagogue,
the challenge was to help them forget what they thought they
knew. Several students were convinced that the biblical Isaac
was a young boy at the time of the story of the Binding of
Isaac. This perception was based on Rembrandt's portrayal of
Isaac as a young child, but his age is not clear from the text — in
fact, it is more likely that he was in his thirties during that fate-
ful episode. This small detail crystallized for me the ways in
which familiarity breeds blindness. One of our jobs as educators is to help students forget what they know so they can stay
alert to the texts' nuances.

Professor Wiesel sought to create dialogues between the lit-
eratures of many eras and cultures, using one tradition to shed
light on another. In examining the Binding of Isaac, he turned
to the character of Iphigenia in the plays of Euripides. To help
us really see Joseph in the Bible, he had us study his portrayal
in the Koran. When we studied the book of Job, with its sudden appearance of God, the professor had us read the Bhagavad Gita to better understand theophany in literature. In order
to help us grasp Sophocles, he had us read Brecht, Kafka, and

Camus. And this comparative approach to learning extended to the students themselves.

In class we are discussing the theme of revolution and the transformation of radical movements into rigid establishments. Professor Wiesel describes the origins of the eighteenth-century Hasidic movement, its roots in Eastern European Jewish mysticism, and the lives of its founders. I don't expect the conversation to become heated.

He speaks in a low voice and seems to be focused on a distant place. "Does Hasidism recognize change? Yes—and no. The movement itself changed; it was at first revolutionary. Then, as a result of its encounter with modernity, it became very conservative. In *reaction* to modernity, the communities of mystical imagination closed ranks, becoming fearful of the outside world, suspicious of anything not found in the old texts. From its origins until the later masters, Hasidism is totally different. Why? Because the world changed. Today, it's not easy to be a mystic."

Then he turns his attention back to the class. "We are discussing a Jewish religious movement. How do you *Christians* feel here, reading these tales, learning this history?"

Olivia, a grad student from Poland who has already fallen in love with all things mystical, sighs and says, "I feel I found a truth I've been looking for, a gift."

A theology student, Matt, says, "So much of this, the rebbes and their teachings, reminds me of Jesus—the charismatic leaders, their suffering on behalf of others—"

An Orthodox woman, Chaya, is offended. "I don't like when people make that comparison. I come from a Hasidic family. Where do you think Jesus got his ideas? From Judaism!"

A fierce debate ensues about whether it is legitimate to describe one religion, one truth, using the language of another. Isn't it messy to mix and match intellectual frameworks, to use modern psychological concepts to describe premodern experiences of suffering, for example? And yet, don't those modern scientific categories help illuminate those experiences and bring them closer to us? We discuss syncretism—the effort to integrate elements of different religious traditions and practices; for instance, Jews who practice Buddhism. Professor Wiesel cautions us against sloppiness in language and exhorts us to be exceedingly precise in our thinking.

"Remember," he says, "Judaism does not insist the world become Jewish; it insists only that the world become good, each person in his own path. Remember that the Besht"—Rabbi Yisrael ben Eliezer, the eighteenth-century founder of the Hasidic movement—"told one of his followers, 'Beware your coachman. I saw him walk by the church without crossing himself!' He believed that a good Christian would be a good and trustworthy human."

"Really?" asks Park, a Korean minister in training. "But don't Jews put their own people first? Isn't that what the notion of the Chosen People means?"

There is a pause, then Chaya sits up in her seat and says, "I cannot believe you said that. That's such a stereotype!"

"Wait," says Professor Wiesel. "We are here to learn together, and we must listen. How else are we to change others' minds or our own?" Then he turns back to Park.

"The notion of chosenness," he explains, "surely has caused some Jews to fall into the trap of triumphalism. Yet, with one short-lived exception, the Jewish people never tried to proselytize, and Jews did not force others to convert. Just the opposite; they dissuade others from joining them. When someone comes to us wanting to become a Jew, we say, 'Why would you want that? Don't you know that we are the most persecuted people on earth, that we have never had a single generation free of attack?' For a Jew, to be human is to be Jewish. My humanity is expressed through my story, my roots, my tradition. It is the same thing for others. For a Christian, to be human is to be Christian. For a Muslim, to be human is to be Muslim. For a Buddhist, to be human is to be Buddhist. To claim that one path is better than another, to denigrate others, has an almost inevitable outcome: dehumanization."

"What does Chosen People mean, then?" asks Park.

"The word in Hebrew is *segulah,* which does not really mean 'chosen.' It means 'set aside for a special but not exclusive role.' In other words, one may be chosen to serve rather than to benefit, to suffer rather than to be rewarded, and to help others realize their destinies. This is how it is presented in many Jewish teachings. After all, in the very first encounter of the first Jew, God told Abraham, 'Through you will all the families of the earth be blessed.' The vision of Judaism was universal from its inception, and its particularism serves that universal vision. And, in the world of Hasidism, the Besht prayed for 'every mother's child,' not only for his own people. And most of all, remember: Those who fought on behalf of Jewish causes like Soviet Jewry"—Jews who were trapped behind the Iron Curtain, unable to emigrate, and who faced discrimination and often imprisonment for their involvement with religious life—"went on to fight on behalf of Cambodian, Yugoslavian, and Rwandan victims. The more Jewish I am, the more human I am, the more rooted in my identity, the more I can be there for others."

Lewis, a Methodist minister of a church in Connecticut, brings the conversation back to our original topic. "But didn't mainly Jewish people go to the rebbes for blessings or advice? Wasn't Hasidism still a parochial movement?"

Professor Wiesel replies gently, "On the contrary. Many of the masters were known for their appeal to the non-Jewish world as well. The Besht, the great preacher of Kozhenitz, and many others received visitors and had followers from among the general population—peasants, innkeepers, farmers—all coming to ask for blessing or intercession. Later, of course, the Hasidim became more insular—this is not surprising when we consider that half of the Jews murdered in *those years* were Polish Jews, and ninety percent of Polish Jews were Hasidim. But at the beginning it was a very universal, a very human, community. Which is one of the reasons I love it." He says this last with a smile, and I notice that Park is smiling too.

Then Professor Wiesel asks another question: "And how would it feel if this class were reversed, if our Jewish students were attending a lecture on the New Testament?"

Chaya says, "I have never studied the Christian Bible, and I have to be honest that I don't really want to. It makes me uncomfortable to read the book that inspired so much hatred of Jewish people, over so many years. Even that name, New Testament, is offensive to me. It implies that the Jewish Torah is no longer relevant."

I see some of the Christian students bristle at this, then eagerly look to Professor Wiesel for his response.

"You know, I felt this way when I was young. In my little town, we were afraid of Christians. My Christian schoolmates and I had very little do with one another; there were walls between us. And during Easter, which was the time most likely to explode into anti-Jewish violence, we stayed home. We were afraid to go outside! And we felt, many of us, that whatever took place in the churches was a kind of dark threat to us. So I understand your feeling. Nevertheless, later on, when I studied and when I met church leaders and many good people who are Christian, I learned that misunderstanding travels in both directions. I believe we must learn, and we must speak to one another, if we are to have hope of healing what must be healed."

Kathy, an older woman and a graduate student in religion, raises her hand. "Professor, I've wrestled with the Catholic Church's anti-Semitism for many years. I don't understand how it reflects Jesus's teachings at all, and I was taught that he is the model for us to live by. What would you say to someone like me, a committed Christian in the modern world who believes in respecting other faith traditions?"

"Well, if I truly respect you, that means I can learn from you, that you have some wisdom or a sensitivity that I lack. And you mention Jesus. I have been asked many times in interviews, 'If Jesus lived today, what do you think he would say?' If Jesus lived in my time and place, he most likely would have died in a concentration camp. How can we forget that he was a Jew who lived in a Jewish milieu? That his stories were *Jewish* stories, and his family was a *Jewish* family? The distance between us is not as great as we think it is."

Kathy continues. "But don't you feel the distance is still pretty significant? That interreligious dialogue has stalled since

Vatican Two, that now there is at least some level of 'clash of civilizations'?"

Before replying, Professor Wiesel has her explain to the class that Vatican II was the Catholic Church's call to ecumenical dialogue in the 1960s.

"I think dialogue has progressed in many ways," he says. "And yet, Vatican Two itself, the reappraisal of many aspects of Christianity and especially its relationship with Judaism, lacked certain things. First, it should not have limited the dialogue to Jews and Christians. It should have included Muslims as well. We have seen the need for that dialogue, and had it included Muslim representatives, who knows what new friendships and new understandings might have developed? Not to mention Buddhism, Hinduism, and others. But of course this effort did make a difference and continues to be a foundation for new efforts. Which we need."

He waits, letting his words sink in. Then he says, "As for a clash of civilizations, I don't accept the concept as it stands. Fanaticism has accompanied human beings for all of our history. It is a poison that appears anywhere, in any faith, at any time. The fanatic is afraid of confusion; others call it diversity. Each religious tradition has its methods for battling fanatical readings of sacred texts, and these methods determine the destinies of religious communities."

Kathy asks for clarification.

"Every sacred text contains verses, ideas, stories that are alarming and dangerous. 'An eye for an eye' in the Hebrew Bible, 'I came to bring the sword' in the New Testament, anti-Semitic verses in the Koran. In my tradition, the rabbis of the first and second centuries of the Common Era developed methods to contain or sometimes negate the dangerous verses. So, for example, 'an eye for an eye, a tooth for a tooth' was interpreted to mean only financial compensation. Is this the literal meaning of the text? No. But the rabbis had no compunction about interpreting it to neutralize a textual threat. In Judaism, this is called the oral tradition, which balances the written tradition, scripture. Other traditions have struggled with the same issues, with more or less success. These methods of interpreting sacred text determine the future of religious communities, whether they will lead to fanaticism and war, or respect and peace."

Andrea, an activist in interreligious peacemaking, raises her hand. "Professor, I coordinate a group of representatives of twelve religions here in Boston. We have great conversations, but it doesn't feel like it's leading to anything real. Maybe we are too polite with each other. How can we foster conversation that leads to real action and results? And how can we get past the politeness stage of our dialogue?"

"What do you think?" Professor Wiesel replies with a smile.

Andrea is taken aback and says, "I'm really not sure. I try to pick topics that might spark deeper discussions . . ."

Professor Wiesel says, "I think that is good, and really, any dialogue of this kind is so important and much too rare. Nevertheless, it is also good to leave your seats, to go together to actually see what is happening, either in religious environments—go see one another's services, if that is acceptable to the group—or, even better, go see what is happening outside. Go visit the homeless together, go to homes for the elderly or to hospice together. There you will see human beings who simply need kindness, or warmth, or soup. This will take all of the lofty ideas and make them more real, more human."

At the end of this discussion I feel hopeful; this diverse group, several of whom clearly and strongly disagree on important questions, bid each other farewell with real warmth and respect. If it can happen here, why not elsewhere?

Compassion and Conflict

YOU ARE WALKING in a forest. You're lost, it's getting dark, you hear unfamiliar sounds, and you're starting to panic. Suddenly, you hear footsteps crashing through the underbrush. A person steps out onto the path in front of you.

"Hey!" you say. "Do you know the way out of here?"

He looks at you, breathing hard, and says, "I don't know the way out. But I can tell you one thing: *That* way is bad news!"

Professor Wiesel tells this story and laughs. He continues. "That is the story of humanity. We must tell our children: Don't go there — we just came from there. Beckett wrote, 'My mistakes are my life.' In our search for truth, we do not expect to find the answer. But we can help each other avoid dead-end paths. This is why we need each other."

We need each other precisely for our differences and the varied paths we have known, he says. Those differences can cause conflict, and that conflict can be destructive or constructive.

An undergrad named Jacob asks, "What does it take to create constructive conflict?"

Professor Wiesel replies, "First, courage. Our natural tendency is to avoid confrontation, and this can lead to a politeness that, for the sake of learning, must be challenged. This is why I encourage you to question me, to question one another, and to question your own assumptions." Indeed, I've observed that he smiles more when the class becomes a respectful yet charged battleground of ideas.

Wiesel's conception of a battleground demands that we shed our armor rather than use it for protection. When we studied the biblical story of David, he pointed to a powerful moment in the text.

"David, on his way to fight Goliath, was given the king's armor. For a battle this unequal, with life-and-death stakes, armor made sense. But David removed the armor, for it didn't fit him. This image has stayed with me as a symbol of a key concept: that vulnerability is the greatest weapon if you are brave enough to use it."

In spite of his experiences during the Holocaust, Elie Wiesel sheds his armor every day, opens himself up to his students, students he didn't even know, listens to their dreams and hopes, continues to argue for faith and friendship. He says, "Love is possible. Hope is possible." And: "I always teach with an open heart. Not just for moral reasons, but for pragmatic ones — a teacher's open heart makes it possible for students to open their hearts as well."

In class, his willingness to remain open to others, to the moment, helps students do the same. During a student presentation on Brecht's play *Mother Courage,* Daniel, an actor, shares with the class Stanislavsky's method-acting technique.

"By repeating lines from a play while thinking of a painful

moment from my past," Daniel explains, "I can find the emotional charge with which to act out my lines. I'm going to demonstrate with lines from Brecht and real, and very personal, memories."

He reads what is perhaps the most dramatic scene in the play; it comes at its end, when Mother Courage has discovered her daughter's corpse. In a state of denial, world-weary cynicism, and despair, she sings her fantasy, until the reality creeps in.

> *I think she's going to sleep.*
> *Lullaby baby*
> *What's that in the hay?*
> *Neighbors' kids grizzle*
> *But my kids are gay.*
> *Neighbors are in tatters*
> *And you're dressed in lawn*
> *Cut down from the raiment*
> *Angel has worn.*
> *Neighbors' kids go hungry*
> *And you shall eat cake*
> *Suppose it's too crumbly*
> *You've only to speak.*
> *Lullaby baby*
> *What's that in the hay?*
> *The one lies in Poland*
> *The other—who can say?*

Daniel repeats the final lines over and over until he begins weeping openly. (Later he explains to the class that it is sorrow over the death of his uncle that he brings to his reading.) He doesn't wipe away his tears as he reads, and they flow down his cheeks. This is uncomfortable, and so brave, it makes me wish that we could all live with such vulnerability. The room is silent. Then Professor Wiesel, who has been listening quietly from a seat to the side of the room, approaches Daniel, puts his hand on his shoulder, and says a simple, quiet "Thank you."

In the face of opposition, revealing such vulnerability is much more difficult, but it can make the difference between peace and its opposite. Geoff tells the class the following story.

A young mother was walking with her baby down a dark city street when she heard footsteps and realized she was being followed. She walked faster, and the footsteps hastened as well. Then, from the corner of her eye, she saw a man coming toward her quickly and aggressively. As the man approached her, without thinking, she handed her baby to him. The man instinctively responded by taking the baby and holding it gently. All his aggression melted away, and he started rocking the baby and smiling sheepishly.

Professor Wiesel responds to this. "When evil threatens the weak, we must fight back. And yet it is true that sometimes the only way to disarm a threat is to be vulnerable, to share our common humanity, in hopes of awakening the humanity of the other."

Jacob asks what other steps we might take to ensure that conflict doesn't become violent or disrespectful. "There's so much violence all around the world, between groups, nations, religions. What can we do, what must they do, to bring peace? Is peace even possible?"

Professor Wiesel sighs. "It's an old question, unfortunately. And you know, I've been involved in many attempts to create dialogue. We organized conferences. I tried to bring leaders together. The spotlight doesn't help; when leaders have to answer to their more extreme supporters, it is difficult for them to take steps toward peace. War is much more popular. But in private, human connections, human encounters can happen. In 1990 I organized a conference that both Nelson Mandela and a minister from the de Klerk government attended. At the opening of the conference, the minister turned to Mandela and said, 'Nelson, I grew up under apartheid. Now my fervent wish is to attend its funeral.' This small human exchange launched a dialogue that led to the end of apartheid and a new reality for South Africa. How can there be peace in other tormented areas of the world? Through such small, modest, human encounters."

"What about in the smaller sphere of our own lives," another student says, "when you disagree with someone you care about whom you see making the wrong decision. What do you do then?"

This is the kind of personal question I am surprised to hear in a university classroom. It comes from Laura, a middle-aged woman who has returned to college for a degree in theology after going through a divorce. She shared in discussion section that she has a grown son who struggles with drug addiction and who hasn't held a steady job since he graduated college.

Professor Wiesel looks at her for a long moment, then says, "It is very difficult to separate from those we love, those we care about. It is hard to really trust that they have a path that is different from our own. The rebbe of Kotzk said something important. 'If I am I because you are you, and you are you because I am I — then I am not I, and you are not you. But if I am I because I am I, and you are you because you are you — then I am I and you are you.' It is very difficult to allow those we love to be free, to be themselves, to make their own mistakes, create their own destinies. Yet we must—"

"What if we just *know* they are wrong?" Laura insists.

"Remember what we read a few weeks ago, what the Islamic saint al-Hallaj said to his disciple in one of their final meetings. He said, 'Your way is yours; don't imitate mine. You will find your way.' This is hard for any teacher or any parent to say, but it is the greatest gift a teacher can give a student or a parent can give a child."

In a different lecture, this one on *The Death of al-Hallaj*, which recounts the martyrdom of a Sufi holy man, a God-intoxicated figure who perplexes the conservative Muslim religious establishment of his time, Professor Wiesel says, "I love al-Hallaj because he loves others so deeply." He asks students to read from a conversation al-Hallaj has with a close disciple who has visited his teacher in prison. Two students volunteer to read the parts of student and master.

[Ibn Ata, the student] How could this happen?
How could God let the scoundrels rule the world?
The world and the heavens are His, we know
From His eternal Word. A brilliant jurist
Who is jealous, a corrupt vizier
And a slothful caliph, conspire to end
Your teaching and (he says softly) your life.
How do you explain their seeming triumph?

[al-Hallaj, the master] By your word seeming. Scoundrels have
    small goals
For which their lives have set high stakes. My death

Is not momentous as a goal to me
But their continued need for power
Depends on it. Their triumph
May not last too long. It may appear
Much less important when I'm dead.
But scoundrels never think ahead. Longevity
Is useless, for they must work fast.
But there is always someone who is played upon
And one who plays—a scoundrel is two men,
Thus neither thinks he's bad within himself:
Just as a saint is two, two friends
Whom God transforms to one through love. No one
Is saint alone, only self-righteous.

Professor Wiesel repeats the words. "A saint is 'two friends whom God transforms to one through love.' The search for our own holiness, our own accomplishment, so often blinds us to the other who stands before us. Albert Camus in one of his novels asks, Can one be a saint without God? I ask, Can one be a saint without other people? My answer is no. How can you become a saint if you don't notice the homeless person on your way to work, the old woman standing on the bus who doesn't have a place to sit?" He looks around at his students, young and old, from many countries, with many pasts. "If we want to achieve anything good," he says, "we cannot do it alone."

3
Faith and Doubt

If I had not had faith, my life would have been much easier.

— ELIE WIESEL

IN 1997, IN A hotel lobby in Jerusalem, I looked at Professor Wiesel and asked my question: "Is it possible to build a religious life based on doubt?"

A few months earlier, I had decided to take a year off from college and go to Israel to study in yeshiva. In doing so, I imagined I would join a community of seekers who, under the tutelage of spiritual masters, would each fulfill his singular potential. The personal traits with which I struggled—laziness, shyness, desire—would evaporate, and I would emerge as if from a chrysalis, new and whole and ready to serve the world.

I was packing for my trip overseas when my father called me into his room with a strange formality.

He said, "Listen, you're going away for a while, and a lot can happen on these trips." He handed me a pack of condoms. "Don't try to be a saint."

Something in me clenched. "What else is there to try to be?" I answered, and I went back to packing.

Our conversation threw fresh light on the complexities of

my decision. My mother followed the law; my father followed his inspiration. My mother wanted me to know; my father wanted me to feel. My mother wanted me to become a scholar; my father wanted me to be whatever I wanted. As for me, I couldn't ignore the longing I felt, a longing that had started with the wish to find a rebbe and that was slowly but inexorably expanding into a yearning for holiness. My earliest teachers had given me a profound love of learning and religious life, which my subsequent readings in other traditions had only reinforced. What else was there to try to be other than a saint, a person whose being has been transmuted into the stuff of holiness, a transparent lens whose function is to channel light into our world? I believed that, through ardent study and fervent practice, I could become a better version of myself.

After an eleven-hour flight that I spent writing in my journal and listening to my favorite Peter Gabriel album, I arrived in Israel. I remember the ride from the airport to the yeshiva in a chartered van, the fresh smell of jasmine and hot asphalt in the air, and the bright Middle Eastern light over fields, orchards, and vineyards.

The yeshiva was located on a hilltop south of Jerusalem that was filled with scrub and the occasional olive tree. The wind blew incessantly, and the stars at night were the brightest I'd ever seen. All the buildings were metal boxes—the Hebrew word for them translates to "caravans"—that were stacked together or lined up to create larger spaces. I was greeted by an older student named Dov, a redhead with a sparse beard. He told me he'd been studying here for seven years and was planning to stay forever.

Yeshiva is the closest Judaism comes to monastic life. Most

of the students were American kids like me, nineteen- and twenty-year-olds, and there were also some older students like Dov who were studying toward rabbinic ordination. Walking up the hill to the study hall, I often passed young mothers from the nearby town with strollers and head coverings; Arab workers; and, occasionally, an old Jew with a long silver beard riding on a donkey and blasting techno music from a boom box. In September the weather suddenly changed; gray clouds swept in from the coast and brought a coolness in the air heralding a Middle Eastern winter, a season different from any I'd known.

The first months were a whirlwind of new ideas, new friends, and long hours of study. Following the traditional form of Talmud study, we learned in pairs, reading and rereading each line, not to mention the commentaries, written by rabbis across continents, across generations. Consulting an Aramaic-English dictionary, we slowly, doggedly translated a few words at a time, often getting them wrong, being corrected by our teachers in the hour-and-a-half-long class that met before lunch. We were being trained to notice any extra word, any extra letter—the slightest detail had the potential to upend the meaning of a text. If before this I had been on the ground level of Jewish learning, now I found the basement, and then the subbasement—deeper and deeper levels of study.

My new friends were seekers like me. Returnees to tradition, they generally came with profound sincerity and not much traditional knowledge, but they remedied the latter quickly. They were mostly college graduates, but there were also some activists and a few artists, people who had discovered Judaism and were in yeshiva to catch up on what they had missed growing up assimilated in America. Their enthusiasm was contagious, and I was happy to be a part of such a sincere and searching community.

At the same time, I was learning that the reality of yeshiva life was more complicated than I had imagined. Our teachers taught us the technical skills we needed to access the texts, but when it came to philosophy and theology, they offered pat answers that I found neither credible nor compelling. Once, when I asked a particularly difficult question, I heard one of the teachers comment to another, "We've got to pin that boy's wings to the ground."

I became increasingly irritable. The more I tried to change and grow, the more it seemed I was locked into place, stuck with myself and all my weaknesses. In my first few weeks, following the advice of one of the teachers, I had drawn up a daily schedule to maximize study time as well as a chart of character traits I wanted to improve. I lived by these two documents, which left little room for spontaneity or relaxation. I thought of what my mother's father, a serious intellectual, once said to me: "Happiness is not a Jewish value." When I didn't meet my goals for the day or the week, I castigated myself. I stopped replying to friends' letters, called home less and less often.

I continued to surrender to the path set out by my teachers, the one my grandfather valorized when I was young, but often experienced an internal backlash—a sudden cold or flu, days of fatigue, a bewildering surge of anger. Was I betraying myself? Was I being seduced by transcendence?

Several months after I arrived in Israel, someone in Professor Wiesel's New York office called to tell me that he was coming to Jerusalem, and I asked for an appointment.

The following week, I took a bus to the King David Hotel to meet with him. We sat in the sunlit lobby, which was filled with tourists in Hawaiian shirts. Professor Wiesel wore a short-sleeved shirt, the first time I had seen him in anything other than an immaculately pressed charcoal-gray suit.

I wasn't sure what to call him. In college, it made sense to call him Professor Wiesel. But here in Israel, my tongue was tied. He wasn't a rabbi; I couldn't call him that. I thought about using an alternative Hebrew honorific, *mori,* which means "my teacher," but this sounded too formal. I did what many of us do in unclear situations: I awkwardly avoided calling him anything. Nevertheless, I felt I could speak openly with him.

I had thought about my question for weeks, trying to find the best way to express it. "I am wrestling with something," I said.

"Of course—that is really why you came here, isn't it?"

This brought me up short. "I guess so."

And so I asked my question: "Is it possible to build a religious life based on doubt?" If I could find a place for doubt in my religious life, I thought, maybe I could integrate my mother's quest for knowledge and my father's quest for freedom. Doubt, I suspected, could be the protective mechanism by which I could avoid losing myself, a way to step back and examine the answers my rabbis gave, weighing them against my inner moral code. But this was not something I had ever heard from my teachers.

Professor Wiesel thought for a moment and then said, "If it

is doubt together with faith, that is good. It can deepen faith, and make it more real. It is easy to fool ourselves, to think we have more faith than we actually do. Doubt is a kind of inoculation against this."

"I have so many questions," I replied. "And the rabbis in yeshiva give so many answers. But when I hear their answers, my questions only feel heavier than before."

He looked at me for a long moment in silence. Then he said, "You are sincere; I can see that. And these questions come from your sincerity, your seriousness. We all ask questions, and we should. It is more dangerous if we do not. But perhaps you are not looking for answers. You are looking for *responses* to your questions, to your life, for ways to live rather than ideas to espouse. Answers close things down; responses do not."

In the days that followed, I felt my old beliefs peel off like skin after a sunburn. Maybe it wasn't true that faith and doubt were opposites. Maybe my questions actually emerged from faith and served to telegraph the immensity of the subconscious spaces that I had yet to fill with meaning. As I walked through my days, I felt my questions as a comet's tail behind me, marking my crossing, illuminating rather than darkening the path before me.

IN ANOTHER CONVERSATION a year later, sitting in the same spot in the same hotel in Jerusalem, I asked Professor Wiesel about becoming a rabbi. I had entered my course of study with no intention of being ordained, though my grandfather had told me often to "get ordination and put it in a drawer" — meaning that I should become a rabbi but not pursue a rabbinic career. The head of my yeshiva was now trying to persuade me to change my mind. "We need good rabbis," he said, "and besides, this way you can tell your parents you're working toward a degree, so they won't panic that you still haven't finished college!"

What did Professor Wiesel, who had declined to become a rabbi himself, think of this?

"First," he said, "make sure you are serving the master you want to serve and not another. There is pressure to have a career, to serve, but there are many ways to serve. You need to know that you are doing the right thing for you. So listen, and listen well. You have time, so listen. Then you can decide."

"Do you think it's possible to be a rabbi and also an artist?"

"Of course. Because you are an artist, you cannot avoid creating. If you are a rabbi, you will also create, and you can bring those things together. But will your community support you to do so? That I cannot tell you."

"Is that why you decided not to become a rabbi?"

"I declined my teacher's invitation only because I felt my voice, my writing, is my *shlichut*"—Hebrew for "mission"— "and I knew that whatever authority I might have must come only from my words, not from a degree."

I said, "I'm under some pressure to get a degree, or several, soon. But I want to continue my studies here."

"Don't forget to hesitate. Ask whether you're doing something because it's comfortable. The main thing is, make the essential, and the inessential. If you can think about this always and identify what is truly essential . . . the next level is when the inessential becomes *part* of the essential. Otherwise, the inessential starts to creep in and you don't notice."

Then he sighed and said, "Look, you are doing good things

now, and you will do good things later. Just be sure to do them with depth, with sincerity, with fervor. We live in a world of easy answers, quick degrees, careers only for the sake of money." He smiled and added, "Superficiality is the enemy of everything."

Night and Faith

FALL 2006, PROFESSOR WIESEL'S classroom in Boston. "How can we have faith, especially in God, after what happened?" a ministry student named Philip asks in a class on Elie Wiesel's first book, *Night*. An account of Wiesel's family's deportation from his hometown in 1944, the separation of his family, his experience of the death camps, and the loss of his father, *Night* is a classic of Holocaust literature. It is required reading in schools across the world, and when it was published in French in 1958 (after being rejected by seventeen publishers) and in English in 1960, it changed the conversation about the Holocaust, theology, and suffering. Yet it is a book that Professor Wiesel rarely teaches because he prefers discussing Sophocles, Shakespeare, Camus, and Kafka, as well as the Bible and Hasidism. The Holocaust is always in the background; he does not cover it directly. But because his students have been asking him to for weeks, he is now lecturing on *Night*.

Philip is a stocky young man with an intense stare, a Jesuit devoted to academic life and pastoral mission. He recently found out that his mother was Jewish and that as a child, she'd survived the Holocaust, a secret she'd hidden from her family for years. This discovery has clearly shaken Philip's faith in both his mother and his religious identity, challenges we've discussed during my office hours more than once. His question in class is one that is on many students' minds as they encounter the howling void of the Holocaust: "How can we live without faith, and how can we live with it?" It is snowing outside, and the lights in our classroom are fighting a losing battle against the dusk and the sense of desolation it brings. Students have come here hoping to affirm their faith or find sources to support their atheism or get answers to their theological questions. Instead, they are finding only more questions, questions that challenge their faith or lack thereof.

"We cannot understand that period with God or without God," begins Professor Wiesel, looking around the room. His gaze settles on Philip. "Believe me, if I had not had faith, my life would have been much easier. My questions are questions only because of my faith. My argument with God is an argument only because of faith. Sometimes I have wished to renounce it, but I could not."

This statement encapsulates Elie Wiesel's conundrum, his paradoxical faith. Faith and doubt are often on Wiesel's mind. A quick scan of his course titles over the years underscores his focus on these themes: Faith and Heresy, Faith and Power, Faith and Tragedy, Faith and Destruction, to name just a few. He is a religious man who also believes deeply in people, though he has good reason to renounce faith in both God and humanity. His questions about God's role in human suffering drive him. How could God have let it happen? Can one have faith after the Holocaust? Can one have too much faith? What is the relationship between faith and hope, faith and despair, faith and power?

Professor Wiesel continues. "I believe in a wounded faith. Only a wounded faith can exist after those events. Only a wounded faith is worthy of a silent God." What is a wounded faith? In Wiesel's case, it is a faith that began in the small town in Hungary where he spent his childhood, a town called Sighet.

The Faith of a Child

GROWING UP, ELIEZER WIESEL was pious. Filled with fervor and a child's simple faith, he spent his days studying sacred texts, pining for God as for a faraway best friend, and praying for the Messiah to come. Like any child, Eliezer played and lost himself in dreams, but his dreams were populated by characters out of Jewish legend. His dreams were of Jerusalem. "I knew the name of Jerusalem before I knew the name of my hometown. The first lullaby my mother sang to me was about Jerusalem. The first prayers I recited were about Jerusalem," he said. Reflecting these early years, Wiesel's original Yiddish version of Night begins with the lines "In the beginning was faith — which is childish; trust — which is vain; and illusion — which is dangerous."

His dearest wish was to become a great Jewish scholar, perhaps the head of a small academy, a place where the song of Torah study could permeate his days and nights. His parents encouraged these dreams, and his maternal grandfather, about whom he would later write, introduced him to the Hasidic tales he would love for the rest of his days.

The spiritual life of his community revolved around the Jewish calendar, the synagogue, the study hall, and the Hasidic rebbes who lived nearby. Every day, Eliezer woke early, walked to the study hall, donned his tefillin (phylacteries, traditional leather boxes with sacred scrolls inside that are worn on the upper arm and forehead), and prayed. After prayers, he studied: the Bible and its commentaries, the Talmud, Midrash, Maimonides. Professor Wiesel told us in class: "Words were exalted, were holy. Before praying in the house of study, I washed my hands. If a book fell down, I picked it up and kissed it."

Eliezer's grandfather was a follower of the Vizhnitzer Rebbe, known for his love of people, and the young boy occasionally traveled with his mother or grandfather to see the master.

In class one day, a course on Hasidism, he tells a story about one of these visits.

"When I was very young, my mother took me to see the Vizhnitzer Rebbe. Usually it was my grandfather who brought me, but this time I went with my mother. The rebbe smiled at me and asked me questions about my studies, about the Talmud and commentaries I was learning. After we spoke for a while, he asked me to wait outside while he talked to my mother.

"I waited for half an hour, and when my mother came out, she was crying. 'Why are you crying, Mama?' I asked. But she refused to tell me. I wondered, had I disappointed the rebbe?

Did I do something wrong? Though I asked her again, she refused to explain. I learned the answer only years later. But I am not going to tell you, not yet."

Several students protest, demand to know.

"No — you will have to wait, as I had to wait. I will tell you on the last day of class."

Professor Wiesel once told me that as a child, he believed that, through his studies and his prayers, he could bring the Messiah, the total and final redemption of the world. This belief came from the Jewish texts he was studying daily, with their prophecies of a future world of peace and perfection. It came from his innate intensity and seriousness, for he was a serious boy. And it was reinforced by the mores of his small town's religious culture and its teachers, who, quoting the great medieval scholar Maimonides, exhorted their students to "act as if the entire world depends on you." Young Eliezer was fully prepared for the Messiah to appear and carry the townspeople of Sighet to Jerusalem on clouds of glory. Every day of prayer and study was filled with wonder and the expectation of wonder.

Now, in class, Professor Wiesel continues with a story. "When I was a child studying in *cheder*" — the traditional Jewish elementary school — "I arrived home one day and announced with great excitement to my mother: 'Mama, did you hear the news? Sarah is going to have a baby!'

"'Sarah? Which Sarah?' my mother asked.

"'Sarah, Abraham's wife! She's one hundred years old, and she's pregnant!'"

His face softens into a smile as he continues. "I remember how surprised, how happy, I was for these biblical characters. I felt so close to them; I felt that they were my contemporaries. Later, when we reached the story of Joseph and his brothers, we read that Jacob sends Joseph to check up on his older brothers in the city of Shechem" (modern-day Nablus). "Unbeknownst to Joseph, they are waiting to ambush him, to sell him as a slave, possibly to kill him. So I cried out, 'Joseph, don't go there,' desperate to alter his fate, and the course of Jewish history, with my warning. This is how I studied the Bible when I was young, as if the biblical tales were real and were happening for the first time."

As a teenager, he began studying mystical texts with a teacher and two friends. "My father had forbidden that, because mystical texts were considered dangerous, but we were thirsty for secret knowledge." Among other things, they studied the names of angels, each of which had a different power. If one were to recite that name with the proper intention, the angel could be called to the aid of the summoner. The proper word could change your destiny. (In 2006, he took me aside to show me the notebook his nephew had found while going through his mother's, Elie's sister's, effects. The notebook was filled with IOUs from Elie's father's grocery store. In the back was a list of the names of angels. "I believed that by reciting one of these names, I could become invisible. I tried to use this name in Auschwitz, but it did not work.")

Young Eliezer's mystical studies, traditionally forbidden to anyone under the age of forty, had unintended consequences. "After several weeks, one of my friends went mad. He became catatonic and would not speak to anyone. He had to be institutionalized. Now my remaining friend and I continued. A few months after, *he* lost his sanity, and he also lost the power of speech. But I continued. It is strange to say, but had the Nazis not invaded our little town, I am sure I would have lost my sanity too."

Where Is God?

TAKE THE UNADULTERATED FAITH of a young boy, throw it against the flat brick wall of ovens in which human beings are being burned by the tens of thousands per day, and see what happens to that faith.

The public first encountered Wiesel's shattered faith in *Night,* most notably in the scene of the hanging of a young child. As he is watching this scene, Wiesel hears a man asking, "Where is God? For God's sake, where is God?" He writes:

> And from within me, I heard a voice answer:
> "Where is He? This is where — hanging here from this gallows."

In perhaps the best-known passage in *Night,* Wiesel writes:

> Never shall I forget that night, the first night in camp, that turned my life into one long night seven times sealed.
> Never shall I forget that smoke.
> Never shall I forget the small faces of children whose bodies I saw transformed into smoke under a silent sky.
> Never shall I forget those flames that consumed my faith forever.
> Never shall I forget the nocturnal silence that deprived me for all eternity of the desire to live.

Never shall I forget those moments that murdered my
God and my soul and turned my dreams to ashes.
Never shall I forget those things, even were I condemned
to live as long as God Himself.
Never.

But in class, on a cloudy November day, Professor Wiesel
tells his students, "Even *there*, I prayed. I remember, one day,
someone managed to smuggle tefillin into the camp by brib-
ing a kapo with bread and margarine. My father and I woke up
early and stood in line with many others to put them on . . .
We were not obligated to put on tefillin in the camps—according to the law, under such circumstances, one is not obligated. And yet, these Jews risked their lives to perform this
commandment. And I prayed. If I could pray there, it is possible to pray under any circumstance. Does it mean my prayers
were answered? They were not; of course not. My father died.
So many died. But the prayers were prayers nonetheless. Even
an unanswered prayer is a prayer."

Philip asks, "How could you do it? How could you find it in
yourself to pray?"

Professor Wiesel responds: "It is a good question. Every
morning in the prayers, we say, 'With a great love have You
loved us,' and I said it there. It's a part of the prayers, after all.
But then I thought, *Come on, really? A great love? In Auschwitz?
It is impossible.* As I said, we cannot conceive of that place with
God or without God. It is impossible to pray. But I did, and I
said that prayer, because my father said it, his father, his grandfather. How could I be the last?"

Pat traditional formulas evaporate upon contact with the

murder of six million innocents, and in that context, prayer seems impossible. And yet Wiesel prayed, and in his prayer, we hear the tension at the heart of his faith, the absurdity of which is matched only by its necessity.

A Faith with Teeth

YET THE DESIRE FOR continuity goes only so far. After the war, when a parentless and stateless Elie Wiesel entered an orphanage in France, he returned to the outward religious practices of his youth. "Somehow I closed the paragraph and said the same prayers I had said as a child." But his prayers had changed.

Caught between the impossibility of maintaining the faith of his childhood and his inability to renounce it entirely, Wiesel sought a new kind of faith. Over time, it became something else: an angry faith, an activist faith, a faith with teeth.

In class, Professor Wiesel tells one of his favorite stories.

"During the expulsion from Spain, a family escaped into Morocco, into the desert. They faced the blazing sun, hunger, and disease. The mother was the first to die. So the father dug a grave and said Kaddish"—a prayer acknowledging God's greatness even in the face of death—"with his two children. Then the older child died. The father dug a grave and said Kaddish. Then his *younger* child died. The father dug yet another grave, and then he spoke to God. He said, 'God, I know You want to test me, You want to see if I will lose my faith, if I will despair. I will not! In spite of You, and for You, I will not!' And he said Kaddish."

Wiesel lets us feel the silence the father might have felt, then comments, "God's silence is an old problem. But the father in this tale has a new response: faith as protest, loyalty as an act of rebellion. This is what I call wounded faith."

He goes on: "Kierkegaard wrote that faith must be lost and found again. I replace the word *lost* with *wounded*. At one point in our life it must be wounded in order to be true. One Hasidic master said, 'No heart is as whole as a broken heart.' I believe that no faith is as whole as a wounded faith."

Wounded faith and protest are themes central to Job, Professor Wiesel's favorite book of the Bible. The book begins with a wager between God and Satan over the life of a righteous man named Job. Satan bets that if Job loses his good fortune, he will curse God, while God believes that Job will remain steadfast in his righteousness. Job loses everything: his wealth, his health, even his children, yet he refuses to curse God. The stakes are raised when Job's friends arrive to comfort him. Their "comfort" takes the form of theological justifications for his sufferings based on the biblical teachings (especially in Deuteronomy) that people are rewarded for good deeds and punished for bad. "You must have done *something* to deserve this suffering," they say. But Job disagrees, insisting on his innocence, demanding that God appear to explain what has happened to him.

In the end, God does appear, in a whirlwind, but does not explain anything. He speaks of cosmic mysteries and humanity's smallness and Job's inability to understand the universe and his own life. In the book's final passage, God says to Job, "Pray for your friends who spoke ill of Me." Apparently God does not approve of even biblical justifications for other people's sufferings.

Professor Wiesel and I discuss this last point over many weeks, and when I refer to it as "God's blasphemy," he smiles. "I agree with you," he says. "Job is, after all, part of the Bible, included in the canon, almost as if to ensure that we do not take the earlier theology of reward and punishment too far, that we do not make it a weapon. We can use it to try to understand our own suffering but not the suffering of others."

Job was Professor Wiesel's favorite book of the Bible because it spoke so deeply to his own experience — Job, whose inexplicable suffering foreshadowed that of Wiesel's generation and whose demand for justice gave Wiesel ammunition for his own quarrel with God; Job, whose refusal to concede God's victory and his own guilt forces God to become visible. Wiesel began teaching the book of Job to other orphans like himself when he arrived in France. He later told me that the experience of wrestling with this difficult text with other young people so soon after the war was crucial to his growth as a teacher.

Arguing with God

IF, AS WIESEL FAMOUSLY claimed, the opposite of love is not hatred but indifference, then even when we cannot avert tragedy, we must at least protest it. If the source of suffering is a tyrant or a faceless government, we must engage in political protest. If the source of suffering is God, we must protest against God. How can such protest be an expression of faith?

This form of protest has its roots in the Bible itself. In class we examine the biblical tale of Abraham and Sodom. God has let Abraham know that He intends to destroy the wicked city-state, a place where torture, according to rabbinic commentators, was a regular occurrence and hospitality a crime. Abraham proceeds to haggle with God on behalf of the people of Sodom.

> "Will You sweep away the righteous with the wicked? What if there are fifty righteous people in the city? Will You really destroy it, and not spare the place for the sake of the fifty righteous people in it? Far be it from You to do such a thing—to kill the righteous with the wicked, treating the righteous and the wicked alike. Far be it from You! Will not the Judge of all the earth do right?"

Abraham continues to argue that even forty-five righteous people are sufficient to save the city, then forty, and so on. Professor Wiesel comments: "In earlier sacred texts—Gilgamesh, the *Enuma Elish*—the gods acted on humankind without mercy or care; they played favorites; the hero survived and conquered while the others drowned. Even in the biblical story of Noah, he survives, his family survives, but the world drowns. Noah does not play the role of intercessor. And here we have a man, flesh and blood, an exile, a wanderer, taking God to task for His injustice.

"And yet, do not forget that God invited Abraham to play this role. It's as if God turns to us, the readers of the future, and says, 'I'm going to tell Abraham what I intend to do to So-

dom so that he will argue with Me. I want to lose this argument.' God is in an argument with humankind, and God wants
to lose. We are invited to argue, to disagree publicly and loudly,
with fervor. We learn from this that if you have to choose between God and man, you must choose man — God can take
care of Himself."

Professor Wiesel continues. "Abraham reminds us of Prometheus, the Titan of Greek mythology (and Aeschylus's play)
who disobeyed Zeus and gave fire to mankind. Except the Titan's sentence — an eternity of torture — indicates a very different ethos. Some gods demand obedience. The biblical God
does too but secretly wishes for more than obedience — He
wishes for human autonomy, for a partner with which to enter
into a relationship."

For many of us, it is hard enough to share an unpopular
opinion at a dinner party, let alone demonstrate against God.
It takes a character trait the Hasidic rebbes called "holy chutzpah," and Abraham had it. So did Moses, who protested God's
threat to destroy the Israelites, saying, "If You do this, erase
me from Your book." Centuries later, some Jewish leaders continued to promulgate this value, notably the Hasidic master
Rebbe Levi Yitzchak of Berdichev, who, more than two thousand years after Moses, publicly put God on trial. Professor
Wiesel recounts the story for his students.

"It was Yom Kippur, the holiest day of the Jewish calendar.
Rebbe Levi Yitzchak of Berdichev was leading the service, and
he paused in his prayers. Looking upward toward the heavens,
he cried out, 'God! Today You judge all Your creatures, both
great and small. But I, Levi Yitzchak, the son of Sara Sasha,
I proclaim that it is You who will be judged today! Your chil-

dren are suffering, and You let it happen! They are hungry, they are ill, they are persecuted and even massacred, and You watch in silence!' After this outburst, he returned to the traditional prayers. One may revolt against God as long as it is on behalf of one's fellow human beings."

In Auschwitz, three rabbis put God on trial. They argued the case, both prosecuting and defending God, and found God guilty, and then one of them said, "The court case is concluded; now it is time for the evening prayers." And they prayed. Wiesel saw this with his own eyes and transmuted the moment into his play *The Trial of God*.

"It is possible to argue, to protest, to shout against God, *for* God," Professor Wiesel tells his students. "Indignation may in fact be the most authentic expression of faith, for it is a testimony to our belief—in spite of what we see—that God is just. And even if He is not, we shall still demand justice."

Though the practice of arguing with God is an ancient part of the Jewish tradition, I began to appreciate it only through the eyes of the many Christian ministry students in Professor Wiesel's courses who stayed behind after class to tell me that this concept was so radical, so empowering, that their views of religion—and their own future ministries—were forever changed.

White Fire on Black Fire: Reverence and Critique

ONE OF THE MOST important changes these students were experiencing was in their relationship with sacred texts. Professor Wiesel's story of reading the Bible when he was young ("Sarah is going to have a baby!") was not only a moment of joyful imagination, it was, in an important sense, the foundation of how he related to texts throughout his life. Just as his faith compelled him to quarrel with God, somehow holding the tension between reverence and critique, the seriousness with which he took scripture caused him to demand justice from those texts.

Sacred texts, which were taken at face value by millions of believers, were, in Professor Wiesel's words, "theological plutonium": dangerous, delicate, capable of causing conflagration when believers turn to violence based on their interpretation of scripture. Scripture influenced the Founding Fathers and Martin Luther King Jr. It has also provided source material for racists and genocidal tyrants.

In class, Professor Wiesel discusses Genesis, chapter 9, which recounts how Noah, after surviving the Flood, planted a vineyard and became drunk. Professor Wiesel generally lectures bareheaded. But when he wishes to quote a sacred text like this one, he pulls a yarmulke out of his jacket pocket and places it on his head. Then, when he is done quoting scripture, he takes it off again. Sometimes this gesture is repeated many times as he moves from sacred to secular texts. ("Why doesn't he just keep it on or take it off?" students ask me. "Because neither one alone reflects the totality of who he is," I answer.)

Noah's youngest son, Ham, enters his father's tent and sees Noah lying naked on the ground, inebriated. He tells his brothers of what he had seen, and his brothers, Shem and Yaphet, enter the tent backward and cover their father's nakedness. When

Noah awakens, he curses Ham (actually, he curses Ham's son Canaan) to be "a slave of slaves." Because Ham and Canaan are associated in biblical commentaries with Ethiopia, this story was used as an argument in support of slavery. Throughout the southern United States in the 1860s, one might have heard this text quoted in Sunday sermons.

I am disturbed by this. But I am appalled a few weeks later, when, in Professor Wiesel's other course, titled Literary Responses to Oppression, I discover a more contemporary consequence of the tale of Ham. We are discussing Philip Gourevitch's *We Wish to Inform You That Tomorrow We Will Be Killed with Our Families*, which describes the 1994 Rwandan genocide. Gourevitch devotes a section of his book to the role of Christian missionaries in creating the racism-infused culture in which the genocide could take place. He points specifically to the Hamitic myth and Noah's curse on Ham's descendants. This text was used by Belgian missionaries as a basis for a racial theory that pitted Tutsis and Hutus against each other, which led indirectly to the 1994 genocide; Hutus lashed out at their Tutsi neighbors, murdering more than eight hundred thousand people in one hundred days.

On Monday morning in Professor Wiesel's class we read Genesis, analyze its themes, and explore its commentaries. On Tuesday, we learned that the very same text had been a force for unspeakable horrors. What can we do to ensure that sacred texts are used to create a world we want to live in?

In our weekly meeting, I ask Professor Wiesel about Genesis and Rwanda and the challenge of finding an ethical way of interpreting holy books. "This is a problem the ancient rabbis already identified," he says. "They taught that the Torah itself can be either an elixir of life or a poison, depending on how it is used. If it is made into a weapon, it is the worst weapon of all."

"But if we prefer an interpretation, even for moral reasons, does that necessarily make it true? What if it contradicts the simple reading of the text? And if it is true to the text but is immoral, what are we to do?"

"If even the most authoritative teaching, the most sacred text, leads to dehumanization, to humiliation, to harm, then we must reject it. Remember, the Bible itself shows us how to do this: Abraham argues with God on behalf of Sodom. Moses breaks the tablets of law—yes, even the law must be broken when it threatens humanity. Job refuses to accept easy answers that falsely render him a sinner and God a vindictive god. We need courage in reading scripture, courage and compassion. Remember also: This is what the rabbis did with so many of the legends they taught, so many interpretations. They worked to align the text with their moral understanding. And in doing so, they gave us permission—no, an obligation —to do the same."

I think of our conversation so many years ago in Jerusalem. "We all ask questions, and we should. It is more dangerous if we do not." I realize now that he was preparing me, empowering me to dive into yeshiva, into faith, study, and practice, but not to abandon my inner sense of right and wrong. Like a swimmer who hasn't been taught any strokes, I had begun my yeshiva study by jumping into the deep end of a vast pool. Until Professor Wiesel and I met in Jerusalem to discuss faith and doubt, I was floundering. Though I didn't realize it at the time, he was teaching me to swim.

Now our discussion about Genesis and Rwanda continues, and I begin to understand his approach. When we encounter difficulties in the text, when we feel the distance between words on a page and our deepest moral intuitions, we allow the text to question us; perhaps our intuitions require refining. At the same time, we begin to challenge the text, to demand that it live up to our ethical instincts. When a text disappoints us with an anti-human message, we will avoid the sin of premature forgiveness, of letting the text off the hook too easily. A biblical verse seems to condone hatred? *Well, it's an old book, after all, from a different time,* we might be tempted to say. But our role in reading sacred scripture is to ask two questions: "What does the text say?" and "Who may be harmed by this text?" In seeking an ethic of interpretation that remains true to the text and to our lives, we need to balance fidelity with conscience.

In one class, discussing Kierkegaard's famous work *Fear and Trembling,* he explains Abraham's willingness to sacrifice his son Isaac as an expression of faith. "I could never accept Kierkegaard's formulation of 'the suspension of the ethical,'" Wiesel says. "Faith must never be a weapon against human beings . . . but it can be used as a weapon against God, for the sake of God."

"A weapon against God?" Philip looks dubious.

In response, Professor Wiesel introduces a concept from Jewish mysticism that describes the sacred texts as written in black fire on white fire. The white fire is the territory of moral intuition, the place in which our deep sense of rightness takes root. Students often assume that this is the least important part of learning, that the words on the page are essential while their own responses are not. Wiesel insists this is untrue. "Our job," he says, "is to write *our* questions, *our* commentary, in *white* fire on *black* fire."

In discussion section, it is clear that Philip and other students need help understanding this point. Fortunately, Professor Wiesel's own writings help. I hand out copies of his radical reinterpretation of the Binding of Isaac, found in his book *Messengers of God*. According to Wiesel, Abraham's acquiescence to God's command is in fact an act of protest, an ironic obedience:

> As though Abraham had said: I defy You, Lord. I shall submit to Your will, but let us see whether You shall go to the end, whether You shall remain passive and silent when the life of my son—who is also Your son—is at stake!

These are not the words of a compliant interpreter of scripture; they are the words of a rebel. The person of faith is playing a game of chicken with God, waiting to see who will falter first.

> And God changed His mind and relented. Abraham won. That was why God sent an angel to revoke the order and congratulate him [as opposed to God appearing directly to Abraham, as He did earlier]; He Himself was too embarrassed.

In Wiesel's formulation, the role of a person of faith is to do nothing less than defeat God in a contest of ethics, again and again.

God Is in the Question

IN A LECTURE ON *Darkness at Noon*, a novel by Arthur Koestler about the show trials in the Soviet Union, Professor Wiesel explores a different facet of faith. "We human beings have a need for faith, as we have a need for food or water. When we remove God as the object of our faith, we tend to automatically or unconsciously replace God with something else. This is what happened with the two powerful social movements of the twentieth century. Fascism replaced God with the dictator, and Communism replaced God with the idea of history. That is why in this novel about the excesses of Communism, the movement is described as 'a dogmatic cult' with a 'catechism' in which the dictator is a high priest serving the god History."

"But why does it matter which idea or principle we place in the God spot?" asks a student named Irene. "Can't any idea serve as a rallying point, a North Star, for a society?"

"True, any faith can lead to fanaticism. But the biblical idea has one advantage. God's name is never pronounced, as if to teach us that true freedom is to be a servant of the ultimate, the ineffable. To serve anything else, anything limited, no matter how lofty, is to become a slave. And slavery leads to fanaticism, and fanaticism leads to heresy, to martyrdom, to death. History shows this again and again, and social movements founded on even the most noble principles must be judged by their practical outcomes: Do they lead to justice, to kindness, or to executions behind the walls of prisons?

"I love the martyrs, like Giordano Bruno, the sixteenth-century scientist and philosopher who said, 'Light is God's shadow.' I love Joan of Arc, al-Hallaj. I do not love those who *make* martyrs out of some misguided faith. Fanatics and heretics both have faith. Except fanatics have no doubts, and they should. To be human is to doubt. The Hebrew word for 'question,' *shelah*, contains the word for 'God,' *El*. God is in the question."

Suddenly I remember that years earlier, in Jerusalem, Professor Wiesel said the same thing to me. How could I have forgotten? This statement gave me the strength to resist my own modest version of fanaticism, the temptation to substitute transcendent ideals for my own reality.

ANOTHER MORNING, ANOTHER LECTURE, this one on *Waiting for Godot*. Professor Wiesel talks about faith and despair, faith and absurdity. "Is it absurd to wait for the one who never arrives? What happens to the world in the meantime? Does our waiting become a blessing for the world, for others, or does it cause us to neglect them?" He reads Beckett's lines:

> Was I sleeping, while the others suffered? Am I sleeping now?
> Tomorrow, when I wake, or think I do, what shall I say of to-day? That with Estragon my friend, at this place, until the fall of night, I waited for Godot?

"What shall *we* say?" he goes on. "Are we sleeping while others suffer? Does our faith cause us to fall asleep? Or does it wake us up? In the Jewish tradition, we are waiting, always waiting, for the Messiah. But this waiting is not meant to blind us to the world; we are meant to bring the Messiah through our actions. I believe in messianic moments, moments of grace, of understanding, of reconciliation between people. The Messiah is a question, not an answer; a demand, not an excuse; a beginning, not an end."

ANOTHER LECTURE, THIS ONE on a collection of stories about the Hasidim during the Holocaust, by Yaffa Eliach. A grad student named Jennifer asks Professor Wiesel whether he believes in miracles.

"Miracles? For some, and not for others? I feel that for every miracle story, there is an equal and opposite blasphemy, someone who was not saved. I don't like miracle stories, especially in that time, that place. It implies God's selective compassion, something I will not accept."

Often in class, during lectures on the literature of tragedy or the absurd written by authors from antiquity or modernity, he will suddenly ask, "And where is God in all that?"

Occasionally he will say, with some humor, "Come on, Mr. God, really? Why did You do that?" When he says this, some religious students chuckle nervously; others simply laugh.

DURING THE FINAL MEETING of his course on Job, Professor Wiesel leads an open discussion about faith, God's seeming injustice, human suffering, and hope. He begins with questions: Has Job forgiven God? Is there a message contained in this strange and disturbing book, and if so, how can we unlock it? Can anything justify even a moment of human suffering?

Students add their own questions, for this is the last class, and the floor is open. Anna asks, "I know we've discussed this, but how could God wager with Satan over a person's life, and how can this story be a part of the Bible?"

Geoff says, "Reading this on its own is so different than reading it when actually dealing with suffering. As a premed student, I've been in the room with people suffering from terminal illnesses, and in the face of that, I just can't accept any explanation—from the Bible or anywhere else—for suffering."

"Ah," Professor Wiesel says with a sigh and a smile, "then you have learned something important. All of the abstract answers to human pain, any of them can sound convincing—until you suffer, or meet someone who is suffering. And after all, isn't the encounter with another's suffering a form of suffering itself? Don't you suffer, Geoff, when you see someone else in pain? Therefore, the answers go away, they cannot stand in that moment. And this is how we must judge such answers—do we find them compelling even when we are in pain? If not, we must reject them. If this inspires a crisis of faith, then so be it.

"According to my tradition, God also experiences such vicarious suffering. When God sees His creatures in pain, He is in pain. *Imo anochi b'tzarah*, 'I am with him,' the person who is suffering or humiliated, in his pain. In one sense, God is alone, terribly alone, and in addition to being all powerful, God suffers every blow, every ache, of every child in the world. Even as I demand justice from God, I feel compassion for God."

He tells us that his teacher Saul Lieberman once asked him, "Who is the most tragic figure in the Bible?" Wiesel had said, "Maybe Adam, because he was the only man, the lonely man. Or Abraham, who was asked to sacrifice his son. Or maybe Isaac, who was almost killed on the altar by his father." Lieberman said, "No, no." So Wiesel asked him, "Who is it?" Lieberman said: "God. Because God looks down and says, 'I gave you such a beautiful world; what have you done with it? What are you doing with it?'"

Alyssa says, "To me, the book of Job is God's confession. It's not meant to make us feel okay."

Blanche, a retiree and a religious Jew, says, "I can't accept that! I know Job's friends' explanations are rejected, but this is part of the Torah, so there *has* to be an answer. It can't be there just to shake up our faith!"

Anna turns to Blanche and asks, "Why not? Maybe the author trusts us not to lose our faith even when we see this ugly story."

"Maybe your faith is stronger than mine," replies Blanche, "but I can't sleep well knowing that my God can do such things."

A theater major named Dennis says, "The book of Job sets up a choice: either Job has sinned, or God has. Whose side do you take? This is good theater; it makes you *have* to choose a side. You can't go on the way you were before reading it."

But Blanche is not satisfied. "What kind of choice is that," she asks, "and how can anyone choose their own idea of morality over God? Isn't God our source for what is right?"

Now several students have their hands up, clearly agitated by this traditionalist argument. Alyssa does not wait to be called on. She does not raise her voice, but we can all tell she is working to control herself.

"I don't believe that," she says. "Why would we be born with an inner sense of right and wrong if we're not supposed to use it? And it's wrong to make someone suffer as part of a bet. If this happened in a school, we'd call it bullying and we'd call the student's parents into the principal's office. Why shouldn't we expect the same level of morality of God?" Then she adds, "This is why I'm not religious, even though I was raised in a religious family. It's too much to ask of us to let God off the hook when people are suffering so much."

Professor Wiesel lifts his hands, and all attention is back on him.

"I know this is troubling," he says gently. "It troubles me too. And you know, this is why I have argued with God for so many years. It is important and good that both of you are troubled in *different* directions—this is the conversation I wish would happen more often. Believers and challengers to faith together can come to a kind of deeper understanding than either one alone if they listen to one another."

Then, turning to Alyssa, he says, "I sympathize with your perspective. Even from my tradition, the Jewish tradition, which of course is the context for Job, there is a strong critique. You know, in the Talmud, the rabbis teach that someone who plays dice, who gambles, cannot give testimony in court. We don't trust someone who gambles. And here, *God* gambles! God is a dice player! He plays with human *life,* of all things! God would be disqualified from testifying in court! So your problem has echoes, antecedents."

Turning to Blanche, he says, "And I identify with your faith as well. It is the faith of my childhood. The question is, can our faith survive such encounters, such questions? Do they deepen our faith or break it?"

Then, returning his gaze to the class as a whole, he says, "A quest is never in vain. It is possible to read Job as a challenge to faith, as a kind of blasphemy that is part of faith. It is strange that Job is part of the biblical canon. Didn't those who included it realize what it would do to readers? Of course they did, and that is why they included it. It is also possible that by reading Job, we learn . . . how to wrestle with God. Perhaps God does not want us to be passive; perhaps God wants us to fight, to argue, to question. Remember that survivors, both those who believed before and those who did not, were changed by their experience. This is what I have tried to teach you this semester: to question. If you have faith, question it. If you have doubt, question it. Whether you have certainty or uncertainty, question it. And the questions will lead you higher. This is, after all, what we are here to do . . . together."

"A QUEST IS NEVER in vain." When I heard him say this, I thought about my time in yeshiva so many years earlier. I exerted so much effort trying to be a saint that I'd forgotten: Experience is God's way of communicating with us. Our personalities, our intuitions, are not things to be discarded or transcended. Our questions are not impediments to faith; they *are* faith. I realized that, in those early years of my relationship with Professor Wiesel, he gave me a way not only to be in yeshiva, but also to reconcile myself with the values of my parents, two holy, flawed, and beautiful human beings.

A few weeks after the end of the class on Job, I met Professor Wiesel in his office to plan next year's course. Sitting across from me, he began, as he usually did, by asking how I was and whether I needed anything. After discussing my choice of career paths with him for almost an hour, I said to my teacher,

"You give me so much of your time, so much support. Is there anything I can do for you?"

He looked at me with his faint smile and penetrating eyes. "Just *be*," he said. "Just be."

The End of the Story

DURING THE FINAL MEETING of his course on Hasidism, Professor Wiesel leads the usual open class in which students are invited to ask questions about whatever they want.

Finally, Jane, an educator who audits Wiesel's classes every other year or so, raises her hand. "Can you tell us the rest of the story?"

"Which story?" he asks, smiling. He knows which one.

"The story about the Vizhnitzer Rebbe and your mother crying!"

"Ah, yes. I owe you that ending, don't I?" And so he tells us.

"You remember that, after she met with the rebbe, my mother was in tears and would not tell me why. Many years later, when I was already living in New York, I received an urgent message from a doctor in Florida. My cousin was in the hospital and refused to go into surgery without my blessing. The doctor was calling to convey my cousin's request. I was surprised that my cousin was asking for me, but naturally I obliged and said the special prayer for healing.

"A few days later, my cousin was recovering, and he called and asked me to come see him as soon as possible. So I traveled to Florida, to the hospital, and went to see him.

"I asked him, 'Why me? Why was it so important that I say the prayer?'

"He looked at me and said, 'Do you remember, when you were a boy, your mother took you to see the Vizhnitzer Rebbe?' I said, 'Of course!'

"He said, 'Maybe you were too young to remember, but I was there. Did you ever wonder why your mother was crying after she spoke to the rebbe alone?' I said, 'Of course, I have wondered my whole life! Why, do you know?'

"He said yes. Then he told me: 'I was in the room, waiting to meet with the rebbe. He spoke with delight of your studies and told your mother that you were doing very well. Then he closed his eyes and said to your mother that you would become a great man among the Jewish people. "But," the rebbe went on, "neither you nor I will live to see it." '"

Jane voices what so many of us are thinking: "What does this story mean to you?"

"It means that, although the world of my childhood is lost, it is still with me. And that the rebbe's blessing and my mother's tears go together, as blessings and tears too often do. It means that faith can coexist with tragedy, can survive it, and that we carry it with us in spite of —or perhaps because of— our wounds."

4
Madness and Rebellion

We study madness in order to learn how to resist.

— ELIE WIESEL

Night and Madness

IT'S A MONDAY IN October of 2006, the third meeting of
Professor Wiesel's class Faith and Power in Ancient and Modern Literature. Although he began his lecture with a discussion
of the course reading, he is talking about *Night* in response to
a student's question. It seems difficult for him; he pauses more
often than usual and seems hesitant to discuss this, his earliest
book.

"There are things I did not write, that were too terrible to
write," he says. "How could I have seen what I have seen and
remained sane? Years after those events, I asked my good friend
who was also there, 'Did I really see that?' And he said, 'I saw
it *with* you!' It is hard to believe. The mind can hold only so
much absurdity. How did I remain sane? I do not know."

He continues, "The witness inhabits the world of madness.
He sees what is happening with lucidity, but when he reports
what he has seen, he appears to others to be mad. I wrote

about this in my first book, about Moshe the Beadle. He was not mad, but he appeared to be, because who could believe what he had to say?"

A white-haired grad student, Greg, tentatively raises his hand. "Professor, what's a beadle?"

"A beadle is the most humble caretaker of a synagogue," Wiesel answers. "He is a communal servant who makes sure the oil lamps are filled, the sacred books put away in their places. He lives for the community."

Night begins with Moshe the Beadle, a man who has been deported and returned, the only surviving witness to a mass killing of Jews. He is a Cassandra-like figure whose reports of the shootings are disbelieved by the townsfolk of Sighet. Young Elie is fascinated by Moshe; however much Moshe cries out, however often he bears witness, it is not enough. His testimony is ignored. By the standards of the sane townspeople, he is mad, but the reader knows that he is the sane one — it is the world that has gone mad.

"It is illegal to shout 'Fire' in a crowded theater. But if there *is* a fire, it is immoral to remain silent. And in that time, there was a fire," he continues, "so Moshe shouted. One must raise an alarm in such a moment, even though it will be perceived as the act of a madman, even though it makes people uncomfortable. That was the reaction to Moshe. That is often the reaction to a witness."

"Professor, did you believe him?"

"I did not, I could not have; it was too far beyond my imagination. But, unlike the others, I at least *listened* to him, for a simple reason: I loved stories."

Wiesel's meeting with Moshe the Beadle was an early brush

with madness, but it was not the only one. We have already encountered young Elie's two friends who lost their sanity after studying mysticism. And in a lecture, he told us that when he was a child, "each one of us in my family did something on behalf of the community every Shabbat afternoon. My father visited the Jewish prisoners in jail. My mother and sisters went to the hospital to bring something to the Jewish patients. And *my* job was—we had an insane asylum in my little town, and my job was to go there with candy for the inmates. We had to *give* something."

But it was his experience of the Holocaust that cemented his sense that the world was prone to madness. He discusses this during lecture: "The collective political madness of the twentieth century, in the forms of fascism and Communism, took over nations; millions of people were swept up in it . . . How can we protect ourselves against this kind of madness? This is not just an abstract historical question. All roads lead back to Auschwitz. If there is violence today, suicide, mental illness, it may well be because seventy years ago, the world did nothing while six million innocent people were slaughtered. How can that not affect us? Confronting those events is essential in ensuring that our fate is not a malediction."

IN ANOTHER LECTURE a few weeks later, this one on Kafka's *The Trial,* Professor Wiesel is discussing indifference and its antidotes. He leans on a small wooden chair as he speaks. "The apathy of the court officials and other characters throughout Josef K.'s trial allows the proceedings to degenerate into absurdity and terror. In life, too, if you look away from suffering, you become complicit, a bystander. Silence never helps the victims, only the victimizers. If you *do* look, you risk madness. Faced with such a choice, madness is the better option. It is a better option because at least you will not be on the side of the killers.

"There are many types of madness," he continues. "There is clinical madness, which is destructive and which isolates and separates people. In its collective form, there is political madness, when nations give in to hate and lose their way. And then there is its opposite: *mystical* madness, which is an obsession with humanity, with redemption, with the union of people, with the messianic element in human life. One must be mad to believe that we can make the world better, that we can save humanity, or even a single life. It is unreasonable, irrational. But I am for that madness."

Calvin, a sophomore and campus activist, asks, "What do you mean by political madness?"

"We have so many examples," replies Professor Wiesel. "Especially in the twentieth century. The two mass movements that teach us most about this are Nazism and Communism. Both were products of collective insanity, rooted in individual madness — Hitler and Stalin were both filled with delusion and paranoia. Both suspected and murdered their closest compatriots and allies. Their personal demons led to collective suffering on a scale that is difficult to imagine. In both movements, a kind of hypnosis took place, driven by fervor and hatred. Racial and class differences became more important than humanity, morality, even strategy. Hitler was willing to lose the war if it meant he could kill more Jews. He diverted essential resources away from the front, the battle with the Russian army that eventually determined the fate of the war, so that the extermination squads could accomplish more. This is an example of political madness."

"And mystical madness? How can madness be part of the solution?"

"The ones who recognize the coming of evil, of oppression, are often seen as madmen. They are attuned to a reality that most people do not see, to a vision of a world without hatred, a messianic vision. They live for this vision, and they are so sensitive to whatever threatens it that, unlike others, they react immediately. They are usually the first to raise the alarm."

AFTER THE WAR, WIESEL spent several years studying madness, mysticism, and psychiatry as a student in the Sorbonne and on his own. For Wiesel, madness was not simply a literal, clinical dysfunction. It was a motif, a metaphor, a moral circumstance, one that briefly attracted him as an alternative to human community. In a 1990 essay called "Making the Ghosts Speak," he wrote, "For months and months, for years, I lived alone. I mistrusted my fellow humans; I no longer believed in the word as a vehicle of thought and of life; I shunned love, aspiring only to silence and madness."

The feeling of "disgust with the West" Wiesel described later in this essay led him to study Eastern mystical traditions. In his late twenties, while living in France and supporting himself as a journalist, he traveled to India with only two hundred dollars in his pocket, earnings from his articles in Yiddish newspapers. There he explored Hindu mysticism in ashrams, where he chanted, meditated, and practiced "listening to the stars."

This was years before such journeys became popular among young Westerners, and Wiesel was often the only foreigner in gatherings of hundreds.

Though attracted to the asceticism and intense spiritual practices of those communities, he could not reconcile himself to the indifference to human suffering he witnessed. "I saw people, spiritual seekers and leaders, stepping over the poor and starving in the street. I knew I had to move on," he told us in class. "To choose Nirvana and therefore not help others was not a choice I could make." For him, mysticism could not be separated from compassion, and his search for mystical heights was accompanied by a deeply ingrained, this-worldly ethical sensibility. This encounter led him to an understanding that he had to return to his world, to the West, to face its ambiguities and difficulties. Escape was no longer an option.

But his preoccupation with mysticism continued. It led to his fondness for literary characters whose grasp of reality is tenuous: Medea, King Lear, Faust, Quixote, Joan of Arc, Raskolnikov. For Wiesel the teacher, the extremity of these characters' stories helped to shed light on events of the twentieth century, offering insight into collective madness and its opposite: moral sanity. So he lectured on Euripides's portrayal of Medea, who murders her own children in revenge for her husband's betrayal and society's indifference and is redeemed by Helios, the charioteer of the sun.

"Why? Why is this murderer of her own children redeemed?" he challenged the class. Pointing to other, similar questions of justice, he said, "This question is more important, more fruitful, than any answers we might offer."

He lectured on Dostoyevsky's Raskolnikov, the protagonist of the novel *Crime and Punishment,* and reminded the class
of a letter Dostoyevsky wrote in which he said, "I have a new
plan—to go mad." Wiesel commented that "Raskolnikov's delusion of grandeur, his renunciation of morality and simple
compassion, leads him to murder. He believes that he is not
answerable to humanity. But we all are."

He was drawn again and again to Kafka's characters, people who find themselves alone in incomprehensible worlds of
bureaucracy and suspicion. "Kafka despairs so that we don't
have to," he told one class. "His characters, like Josef K., are
often not redeemed; they are sacrifices to inhumanity. Yet occasionally he portrays resistance. *Metamorphosis* has been understood by many students of Kafka as a portrait of rebellion
through grotesque transformation. Kafka shows us what is
possible when no one resists absurdity and when one does, by
any means conceivable."

He was fond of Joan of Arc, the fifteenth-century French
mystic and martyr, canonized in 1920 and made famous in
George Bernard Shaw's play *Saint Joan.* In one lecture, Professor Wiesel says, "Joan's life of faith and war is simultaneously
inspiring and disturbing. We feel for her suffering, we hope for
her victory, and yet our faith in her depends on the voices she
claims to hear." He asks several students to read parts of one
of Joan's monologues, the one in which she describes her mystical experience.

> It is in the bells I hear my voices. Not today, when they all
> rang: that was nothing but jangling. But here in this corner,
> where the bells come down from heaven, and the echoes

linger, or in the fields, where they come from a distance through the quiet of the countryside, my voices are in them.

[*The cathedral clock chimes the quarter*] Hark! [*She becomes rapt*] Do you hear? "Dear-child-of-God": just what you said. At the half hour they will say "Be-brave-go-on." At the three-quarters they will say "I-am-thy-help." But it is at the hour, when the great bell goes after "God-will-save-France": it is then that St. Margaret and St. Catherine and sometimes even blessed Michael will say things that I cannot tell beforehand.

Professor Wiesel thanks the student readers and continues: "Joan trusts her voices and leads a revolution at their urging. Is this faith or madness? Can it be both — can faith be the act of a madwoman? Can madness be an act of faith?"

During office hours later that same day, Leah, a serious and intense student, comes to see me. "I have never told anyone this," she says, "but ever since I was a little girl I have heard voices in my mind."

I am not quite sure how to respond.

She continues. "I always felt alone until I read *Saint Joan* for this course. Now I feel there is hope for me, that maybe I'm not crazy, maybe this is just a part of human experience, however strange." Leah tells me that the voices she hears, which generally play the role of conscience and moral intuition, helped her stand up to the bullying she saw in high school. "I could have ignored a feeling, but I couldn't ignore the voices," she says. We speak for over an hour about her experiences and about the positive role the uncanny might play in human life.

"So That They Do Not Change Me"

A FEW WEEKS AFTER the lecture on *Saint Joan*, a theology student named Rose raises her hand. "We have studied several characters who are mad in one way or another. But, really, you are teaching us, and others, to be sane, morally sane — to keep our heads and our moral compass. Why do we need to study madness in order to come to sanity?"

"We study madness in order to learn how to resist," Professor Wiesel replies. "Madness holds the key to protest, to rebellion. Without it, if we are too 'sane' by the standards of our surroundings, we can be carried along with the world's madness.

"Listen to a story: One day a just man came to the city of Sodom. He began to preach to its inhabitants, telling them to change their evil ways. He wanted to save them from destruction, a destruction he knew would come as a result of their sins against one another. 'Please,' he said, 'stop your cruelty, stop your inhumanity! You must be kinder to the stranger, to the children of the stranger!' He went on like that for many days, but no one listened. He did not give up. He continued preaching and protesting for many years. Finally, a passerby asked him, 'Rabbi, really, why do you do that? Don't you see no one is listening?' He answered, 'I know. No one will listen, but I cannot stop. You see, at first I thought I had to preach and protest in order to change *them*. But now, although I continue to speak, it is not to change the world. It is so that *they* do not change *me*.'

"This is why we must learn from madmen: because they do not stop, even when others shout at them to be silent. Someone who protests a little, who writes one letter—it's fine, it doesn't make any problems. But someone who never stops is soon seen as an outsider, antisocial, a madman. These are the ones who show us how to effectively resist evil."

Cheryl asks, "How do the actions of these marginal protesters affect the mainstream? How do we make sure they're not just dismissed?"

Professor Wiesel looks at her intently. "Do you remember the tale called 'The Tainted Grain'?"

This was the tale by the Hasidic master Rebbe Nachman that we studied on the first day of class, the story of the king and his viceroy and their decision to eat the grain and enter into madness after marking each other's foreheads as a reminder of their insanity.

"Well," Professor Wiesel continues, "there is another version of this tale, one we have not seen together yet." He goes on to tell the new version. In this one, the king eats the grain and enters the madness of his countrymen, just like in the previous tale. But in *this* one, the king tells his viceroy that there is just enough of the previous year's untainted grain to eat and remain sane. He offers this store of grain to the viceroy and says, "You will remain the only sane person in all the land. But there is one condition. You must leave the palace and wander as a beggar from town to town, from village to village. Everywhere you go, you must shout in all the marketplaces and from all the rooftops: '*Remember, my people, that you are all mad!*'"

Professor Wiesel says, "A madman can be a messenger who forces others to recognize evil. An outsider himself, he reminds others of their madness. This is why I study and teach madness: because only through recognizing its varieties can we become sane."

After a moment he adds, "This is the role of the witness."

Where Is Mephistopheles?

A FEW WEEKS LATER, Professor Wiesel is lecturing on Goethe's *Faust,* the tale of a scientist who, in search of knowledge, pleasure, and power, sells his soul to the devil. Mephistopheles, the devil or his agent, first appears in the guise of a large dog who follows Faust home.

"In many ways, *Faust* hinges on the question of the ambiguity of evil and the task of recognizing and naming it. The German poet Heine wrote, 'Germany *is* Faust,' because he felt that Goethe captured the inner conflict of his nation. When Faust says, 'Two souls are in my breast,' Goethe is evoking the tragedy of modern man, the internal split between rational morality and imaginative desire. Faust wants to be both good and powerful. The character of Mephistopheles challenges any sane person's sense of morality, arguing that through radical action, however self-serving, Faust can achieve greatness.

"Goethe himself celebrated action over all. In a famous scene, he has Faust rewrite the first verse of the book of John, from 'In the beginning was the Word' to 'In the beginning was the Act.' Therefore, if Faust is redeemable (and he is redeemed at the end of the play), it is because he has not only contemplated, he has dared to act.

"But, for me, this is not enough. Faust's dilemma is that without knowledge, we are nothing, but *with* knowledge, we are dangerous. It depends what you do with that knowledge — gratify the darkest impulses, or help your fellow man? This was prescient: Goethe foreshadowed Germany's role in the twentieth century."

Professor Wiesel devotes the rest of lecture to the demonic yet charming character of Mephistopheles. "Though he is revealed as 'the lord of rats, mice, flies,' et cetera — a truly infernal power — at first his nature is hidden. And once his first disguise has vanished, another appears; he seems to be a traveling scholar, an intellectual, one who bears gifts. This portrayal is intentional, and important. It teaches us that evil may appear disguised as good. A Jewish mystic taught that to deny evil is as dangerous as to deny God. Therefore, we must always ask, in any situation, 'Where is Mephistopheles?'"

This question, along with two others, appeared frequently in Professor Wiesel's classroom. He often asked, "And God, where is *God* in all that?," abruptly shifting a conversation about literature, history, or politics to the realms of metaphysics and theology.

He also asked, "Where am *I* in all that?," reminding us that seemingly objective conversations about ideas must eventually direct us to ethical self-scrutiny.

And he regularly asked, "Where is *Mephistopheles*?," alerting his students that unless we name evil — in literature and in life — we risk its ascension. In classroom discussions of literary works, we discovered diverse answers to this question — evil was in one character or another, even in the hero of a work; it was hidden in the appearance of altruism; it existed in the space between actions, in a million small acts of selfishness, even in the participation of the reader.

Among the many questions Professor Wiesel often put to the class was this: Was evil timeless, immortal? Did it precede humanity, or was it born with Adam and Eve? Was Hitler evil before he was führer? Were only the killers evil? What about those who sent them? What about those who watched and did nothing?

"Those who intend evil do not want others to ask these questions," he said, "and the bystanders who watch evil happening avoid such investigation. This is the front line of the battle against fanaticism. The fanatic believes he has all the answers, and he has no questions. I have *only* questions, so I am their enemy. Questions can save us from the certainties that lead to fanaticism. To be human is to ask questions, to ask why, to inquire, to interrogate each situation in a search for the truth, the truth of how we must act. We must face such questions rather than turn away from them; we must unmask and confront evil rather than reduce it to something comfortable. It is not comfortable to name and confront evil, but we cannot be too attached to comfort if we want to make the world better."

IN CLASS THE FOLLOWING week, we discuss *The Diary of Anne Frank*, a book most if not all of the students have read as teenagers. For many, it was their first encounter with the Holocaust. In lecture, Professor Wiesel begins with this: "The first thing we must say is the simplest, really: one who reads this diary cannot not love its author. We love Anne, the romantic, dreamy girl. She is sad, and happy, yearning, innocent, and a beautiful and mature author. Her diary has had an impact beyond all other books of that time. Why is that?"

Stephanie raises her hand. "For me, it's because I could relate to Anne in so many ways. Her hopes and dreams are so . . . *normal* in such an abnormal time."

Sonja agrees and adds, "She is somehow hopeful, and that gives me hope."

Paul says, "I just think she had one of those terrific personalities. She's the kind of person you'd want to spend time with, or date." A few students chuckle. Professor Wiesel looks sad.

"It is true. Her personal beauty, the brightness of her character and personality, shine through. When a great light is put in a dark place, it shines even brighter. And she is in a dark place, for two years. Two years! Without fresh air, new friends, or any new people! Camus famously ended his great essay *The Myth of Sisyphus* with the words 'One must imagine Sisyphus happy.' How could Anne imagine *herself* happy, living in such conditions, hiding, always under threat of death? And yet she does.

"Perhaps," he continues, "there was a trait of hopefulness in this family. One of the striking things about the story after the *Diary* ends is that Anne's father, Otto Frank, did nothing to search for the one who betrayed their family. He chose to build a future rather than to avenge the past."

A student asks, "How did you do that? How did you not give up on the world?"

Before he can answer, another student, Sandra, jumps in: "In my family, we learned recently of a great-uncle's search, right after the war, for his mother, who had been separated from the family. After months of searching, he discovered that she had survived the camps. But he also discovered that she had returned to their hometown a few months earlier, only to be murdered by her neighbors. How can such a story not make us give up on people?"

Professor Wiesel nods and says, "Those stories are very difficult. In Kielce, a town in Poland, and in other places, survivors went back home, hoping to rebuild their lives. And they were killed in pogroms. Men, women, and children, all of them victims, and survivors. One of those murdered in Kielce was a three-week-old baby. It does cause both rage and despair.

"It is natural to feel rage, and there is a place for it. The question is, what will you do with that? Will you begin to lash out or isolate yourself, or will you use it to motivate your protest? If you can channel your anger, it can give you strength to do something good.

"But despair is another thing. Rebbe Nachman said, 'There is no despair. No matter what, do not despair!' He shouted these words two hundred years ago, and we have an eyewitness testimony that even in the Warsaw ghetto, during the war, his followers, the Bratzlaver Hasidim, sang these words and danced. One of them had lost his daughter days earlier. They danced through their pain; they danced knowing it was absurd —but they danced. To renounce despair is an act of will. And it is the only way to continue and be able to confront, to resist, darkness."

He turns back to Sandra and says, "You asked why I did not give up on the world. After the war I did come close to despair. I felt hatred for those who were silent, but I rejected that. Hatred is a kind of cancer, and, unlike anger, it serves no purpose. And I was not willing to give up my soul to hatred and despair.

It was a choice. And my tradition is filled with hope. In spite of three thousand years of suffering and difficulty, it is a celebration. I was fortunate to be born into this tradition of celebration, and that gave me the strength to reject hatred, to reject despair.

"Rather than hate, rather than despair, I chose the path of protest, of rebellion, of refusal to accept human suffering. I have tried to live my life against silence. When victims have no voice, I try to lend them mine. When they feel alone, I try to show them they are not by going to them and by writing and speaking about their suffering. This is not enough, but it is something. Had we, in 1944 in my little town, felt that we were not alone, it would have made a difference. But precisely because we felt alone, no one else ever should."

Returning to the *Diary*, Professor Wiesel says, "Tell me, what do you think is the most well-known quote from the book?"

He waits until several students jump in with paraphrases of Anne Frank's statement about still believing that people were basically good.

"Yes, exactly," he says. "'I still believe, in spite of everything, that people are really good at heart.' But we must remember that the *Diary* ends *before* she entered Belsen. We have testimony of her last days from a woman named Irma Menkel. Her account is a necessary and tragic postscript to the *Diary*. Through her eyes, we see Anne dying of typhus. Would she have written this quote about the goodness of human beings after entering the camp, after seeing what she saw? If she had been able to write in Auschwitz and in Belsen, what would she have said? We don't know. We cannot. Certainly, mentioning that quote without including this epilogue does not give the whole picture. It is more comfortable, but it is not the whole truth."

In discussion section later that day, students want to continue this thread. "I read Anne's diary when I was thirteen, and it changed my life," says an undergrad named Wendy. "I didn't know the end of her story. It's so sad and throws into question my understanding of the diary's message. Maybe there is no hope."

"I don't think that's what Professor Wiesel was saying," replies Sandra. "There is hope, but it can only be real once we confront the worst parts of the story. If we avoid those, we fool ourselves, and whatever hope we think we have isn't real, isn't sustainable."

I encourage the students to raise this point in class next week, and they do.

Wendy raises her hand and says, "Professor, I'm still thinking about what you said last lecture about the *Diary* ending before Anne Frank's time in the concentration camp and her death. It was hard for me to hear this, and I've been feeling sad all week. How can we face unhappy endings?"

"That is part of my job," says Professor Wiesel. "The role of the teacher is to help students confront darkness without despair. And the role of a friend is equally important. The only way to fight melancholy and resist the world's madness is together. And there is one other thing that can save us from despair: laughter. Laughter is useful because it undermines the lies and posturing of dictators. And in moments when we are tempted by despair, it helps us find hope, in spite of all reason.

"One of my favorite Hasidic tales tells of a country that encompasses all the countries in the world. And in this country there is a small town, and this town incorporates all the towns of the country. And in the town there is a street, in which all the streets of the town are included. And on that street is a house that encompasses all the houses on all the streets, and in that house there is a room, and in the room there is a man, and that man personifies all men of all countries, and that man, what does he do? He laughs. I don't think this is a laughter of despair or a mocking laughter. It is a laughter of hope in spite of tragedy."

To the Mountain and Back

AS FOR ME, I had dealt with my own type of madness, a kind of mystical madness that was tied closely to my religious quest. When my father had admonished me years earlier not to try to be a saint, I hadn't understood.

Telling the story of those days isn't simple. That time comes to me almost like a dream, one from which I've woken up and remember only vaguely. I have read that this is one of the signs of trauma, and I think that was one layer — trauma, exultation, a kind of fever.

After that first stint in yeshiva in 1995, I returned to Boston to finish college. I lived with a group of friends on a tree-lined street in Brookline, a neighborhood within walking distance of the university, and I spent much of my free time organizing festive gatherings for twenty- and thirty-somethings. I met and began a long-distance relationship with a woman who lived in Israel, the woman I would marry. I was playing a quasi-rabbinic role in my community, giving classes in Hasidic thought, tutoring friends looking to improve their Hebrew skills, counseling people as they confronted personal difficulties. When my friends started asking me questions I could not answer, I realized it was time to return to yeshiva.

Jerusalem in the late 1990s was still in the midst of a renaissance that had begun in the late 1960s and early 1970s. Thousands of young men and women were returning to Judaism after growing up in an assimilated, materialistic America. Some of them had studied Eastern religions and then discovered their own heritage. Others had backpacked through Europe, and their train tickets included a free stop in the Holy Land. Each story was different, but most had in common a search for community, for meaning, and for spiritual experience. Jerusalem at the time was filled with yeshivas for the newly religious, providing access to the daunting world of Jewish text and the guidance of mentors.

I had briefly considered going to art school like some of my friends, but I felt that spirituality, not art, was the most encompassing, transcendent path. My best understanding was that it was only the life of the spirit that conquered death and meaninglessness. I still believed that I could get rid of the dross to become myself, to become the saint my father had told me not to try to be.

In Jerusalem, I came under the influence of several teachers. Rabbi Abraham was a Hasid who spoke to me about the connection between art, holiness, and sexual purity. Solomon was a young, intense spiritual seeker who defined all of life as the project of bringing God consciousness into the world. (He was also an ascetic, and he would die only a couple of years after

I met him, in part because of his self-denial.) Friends of mine went to visit the small apartment of the Amshinover Rebbe, famous for praying for hours at a time and for his love of and warmth toward people, especially young returnees to Judaism. Others became followers of the Biala Rebbe, who gave specific advice about whom to marry, which house or apartment to buy, which job to take. These charismatics were the latest in lines of succession extending back to the 1700s and the early Hasidic movement I had been enthralled with for years.

That spring, during the holiday of Shavuot, when Jews celebrate the receiving of the Torah at Mount Sinai, I was living with roommates in a beautiful apartment in Jerusalem while looking into different yeshivas. My friend Charlie and I were hired to serve as counselors for a group of Russian-American students on an educational program. The custom on Shavuot is to stay up all night studying and to pray at dawn.

We walked to the Western Wall just before sunrise. Gathered with thousands of others from around Jerusalem, I saw the light. I mean this literally. Everything appeared to be surrounded by a golden halo: people, objects, the air itself. I felt golden light in my chest, radiating outward. And this experience continued for the next five days. At one point, walking on Jaffa Street with Charlie, I asked him whether he was seeing anything strange. The oddest thing was that, when I performed traditional Jewish practices, the light grew noticeably —and consistently—brighter. I thought about Jerusalem syndrome, the documented mental illness that occasionally afflicts tourists in that city. Often, these pilgrims, overcome by religious ecstasy, begin to see themselves as prophetic or even messianic figures. I didn't feel crazy, just exhilarated, and because there seemed to be an empirical element to my experience, I could not dismiss it so easily. I spent the next weeks considering what this might mean and what steps I needed to take as a result. I felt ready to organize my life around that light permanently, whatever it took.

In spring of 1998, I married my wife, Sabrina, in a traditional ceremony at a kibbutz near Jerusalem. Originally from Spain, she was an art student at the prestigious Bezalel Academy and had lived in Israel since she was seventeen. We had met the previous summer when we were both counselors on a program for teenagers, and we had connected over our shared love of Hasidic teachings. We were both focused on spiritual growth, intoxicated by religion. Surrounded by family and friends, we stood under the wedding canopy, my teachers officiating. One of them spoke of the "holy chutzpah" that couples need to enter into such a commitment.

We moved into a small apartment in the center of the Jerusalem with an understanding that I would study full-time for the next several years.

I enrolled in a new yeshiva with a sense of joy and seriousness. This yeshiva was deeply entrenched in ultra-Orthodox life, which included prayer and study at the center, but it espoused a surprising openness to different perspectives. The institution's overarching philosophy was based on the teachings of Rebbe Nachman, which was in large part what drew me there. His emphasis on connecting with nature and cultivating joy and, especially, his insistence that every individual must find his or her own path spoke to me on the deepest level. The yeshiva exhibited a kind of spiritual muscularity; it focused on overcoming limitations through hard work and ferocity of will. I knew that by studying there I would be challenged. But I did not anticipate the emotional cost.

I was grateful to be supported financially in my studies and my practice—the yeshiva offered me a stipend to study there, a common practice for married students who show promise. Unlike my first yeshiva, this one was packed with wild seekers, strong personalities looking for personal redemption. My fellow students were filled with energy; the flipside was that they weren't very good about personal space. Loud, expressive prayer was their dominant mode of worship, while I preferred a quieter, more introspective style.

The yeshiva was south of Jerusalem, over the Green Line —in other words, it was part of a settlement (though one assumed by both sides in several rounds of peace talks to belong to Israel). Most Jewish people I knew, even those who objected to settlement expansion, agreed that this area, known as the Etzion bloc, was uncontroversial. But this settlement was anything but. Founded by fervent religious nationalists, it had no fence protecting it from the threat of Arab terrorist attacks. The theory was that by not having a fence, the settlement would signal strength and intimidation. "Fences invite wire cutters," one member told me. Most of the people who lived in the settlement had moved here to build a life of environmentalism and spirituality, but there were some whose sympathies lay with the radical right wing of Israeli politics.

The school I was attending was distinct from the settlement and had a more progressive and pluralistic approach. Our teachers were interested in issues of feminism, in interreligious dialogue, and in artistic expression. We had weekly lectures and discussions on these and other subjects, as well as visits from religious leaders from across the denominational spectrum. The yeshiva's more liberal approach was a constant source of tension with the larger settlement.

Sabrina and I moved from our apartment in Jerusalem to live in a caravan—a small metal trailer—balanced on concrete blocks at the edge of a cliff. In summer it was unbearably hot, especially for my now pregnant wife, and in winter it was cold, with only small space heaters to create the memory of warmth. When the wind blew (and it almost always blew), our home shook and swayed. I sometimes woke up in a panic, afraid that we would slip off the side of the cliff.

Our first child, a daughter, was born. I called Professor Wiesel from the one pay phone in the settlement to share the good news that I'd become a parent. He said, "Mazel tov!," wished me much joy from my child, asked after my wife, then said, "How are you feeling?"

"Now I feel I have a stake in the world," I told him. "Before, I cared about the world, but what was the worst that could happen—I could die? But now I feel I can't turn away from the world even for a moment."

"Of course," he said. "My son changed me profoundly. Once you bring life into the world, you must protect it by trying to make the world better. Our children show us the connection between ethics and beauty, that it is beautiful to make the world more human."

A little over a year later, our second child, a boy, joined our family. The caravan became crowded, but there was joy in these wonderful new people, and my life felt increasingly filled with meaning and purpose.

Everyone who lived in this community was expected to do

guard duty once a month in a tiny concrete booth at the en-
trance to the settlement. Men were required to undergo a kind
of mini–basic training where we learned how to fire an M-16
and Uzi. I was given an M-16 and two clips, which I kept in separate places at the top of the closet in our bedroom. Once a
month at night, I took the machine gun, trudged up the hill to
the tiny guard booth, and spent three or four hours watching
and listening for movement. Each of us was supposed to keep
the gun loaded, with the safety on, and pointed at a 45-degree
angle toward the sky, in case a shot was fired accidentally.

My friends and I would wake up at midnight to recite the
prayer mourning the destruction of Jerusalem and expressing
longing for the redemption of the Jewish people and the world.
We immersed ourselves in the freezing cold spring on the hill
opposite the yeshiva, an act of purification and renewal. We
went to the woods to commune with God in silence or in our
own words. When we were done, we'd gather to dance in a cir-
cle, singing a wordless melody over and over. Once a week, on
Thursday night, we stayed up until dawn, praying and studying.

I was accessing more advanced, more difficult Jewish texts.
My teachers told me I had the potential to become a serious
scholar. Other teachers had taken me aside at various points
to tell me the same thing, starting with my first-grade rabbi
decades earlier, and this had the effect of feeding my sense of
urgency, and my ego, in ways I would see only in retrospect.

I was learning about the path of Rebbe Nachman, and I
joined the annual pilgrimage of his followers from around the
world to his gravesite in the Ukraine, absorbing like a sponge

the stories about his followers and how they lived their master's teachings.

I spoke to the head of the yeshiva often, especially on Thursday nights at two or three in the morning on the way back from the forest, where we would all engage in our private prayer practice. We would sit in his van outside his home so as not to wake up his sleeping family and have long conversations. He told me there was a path of the scholars and a path of the saints and that I had to choose which one was going to be primary in my life. He told me that you have to travel through a tunnel, letting go of yourself for a time, in order to be transformed, in order to come out the other side changed. In my mind, a vague prescription for spiritual growth began to form: Create and project an idealized version of self, then try to become that. Repeat as necessary.

I doubled-down on this approach, pushing myself to maximize my time in the study hall, to cover more ground in the study of sacred texts, to wake up earlier and sleep less, to eat less and more deliberately. If I was tired, I stood while I studied. If I felt unmotivated, I simply pushed myself harder. I kept track of my progress in journals and evaluated myself weekly to see whether I was meeting my goals or falling short. Every once in a while I wondered whether the spiritual path I was pursuing was a healthy one. It was a deliberate experiment, a conscious renunciation of a spontaneous approach to living. I knew it had great power, but I knew it also had great danger. Still, I wanted holiness too much to let it go.

What came to be called the Second Intifada crept up on us. A shooting attack here, stones thrown at a car carrying children there. Two Israeli soldiers took a wrong turn and ended up in an Arab town, where they were lynched. I watched a funeral of a Palestinian man on TV and saw the dead body roll off the bier, stand up again, and get back on. It was a fake funeral, meant to increase tension and hatred. A local doctor was shot and killed as he was driving from Jerusalem to our neighborhood, and we attended the funeral. A young mother was shot and killed as her husband drove her to Jerusalem. They were studying the Bible as they drove. My fellow yeshiva students and I attended that funeral as well, and we wept at the sight of her very young children standing dazed and uncomprehending.

Meanwhile, Israeli military reprisals, which escalated in 2002 after the bombing of a Passover Seder in Netanya, resulted in the deaths of Palestinian civilians as well as terrorists. The percentage of civilian deaths is still a matter of dispute, but whatever the number, these deaths, in addition to reduced freedom of movement for Palestinians, led to increased suffering and loss.

The settlement's inhabitants were a mix of religious seekers looking for a rural life and defiant believers in the right of Jews to settle in Greater Israel. As violence erupted in the area, some of the local adolescents became radicalized. I got into a heated argument with a teenager who was making racist comments in the grocery store; several older residents stood around us and listened. In the adjoining settlement, several young people whom I'd sometimes seen loafing in the settlement square were arrested for plotting to attack an Arab school and were sentenced to long prison terms. I started to wonder where the hell I was.

As this madness was growing, my wife and I worried about

our family and our friends. We rode bulletproof buses to visit my in-laws in Jerusalem and wondered how it would all end.

I started going to interreligious dialogue group meetings, which brought Jewish, Christian, and Muslim spiritual leaders and students together to study, discuss their respective prayer lives, and build friendships. The idea was that peace would never come from political processes alone; it demanded grassroots relationship building.

Sitting in a conference center by the Mediterranean, a young Gazan Palestinian named Bilal spoke of his family's ancestral home in Jaffa and the difficulties they faced getting through Israeli checkpoints to this meeting. A Palestinian priest named George told me that I was one of the first Jews he'd met who discussed theology with him respectfully. He asked me questions about my Jewish identity and relationship to Israel and told me about the amplified suffering he experienced as an Arab Christian: periodic persecution at the hands of local Muslims and occasional harassment by Israeli border police. A Hasidic rabbi and Sufi master chanted together, arms around each other's shoulders, swaying slowly. I saw that many human beings were suffering, regardless of religion and ethnicity, due to the decisions of politicians.

DURING MY FOURTH YEAR in the yeshiva, I became very sick with some kind of undiagnosed fatigue syndrome. For weeks I couldn't get out of bed, and for months after I felt its effects. Looking back, it seems clear: my body was reminding me to come back to myself. I had been ignoring my own feelings for so long, and getting sick was my body's way of telling me to stop.

One day, after weeks of lying in bed, depressed and immobile, I thought: *What does it mean to trade your sanity for the quest for perfection? What does it mean to barter today's peace for a hoped-for future redemption? Must you ignore the one who stands before you today, keeping your eyes on a Messiah, a lofty ideal, a vision of a perfect self? Isn't this arrogance disguised as piety? Is this really what God wants?*

I began to spend time each day listening for my inner voice, that sense of intuitive resonance I remembered from my earliest childhood. I started to let go of the stridency and urgency I'd been carrying around, trusting that I would find my own path in my own time. I was learning humility, getting closer to the ground. I physically slowed down, walking more slowly from place to place. I began to see life and experience not as obstacles to spiritual growth but as the language God uses to communicate with us. Ironically, I would later come to see that this approach is what the great masters I studied were teaching in the first place. I had been blinded by my own urgencies.

I had always been most at home with a paintbrush in my hand, and I connected my new insight to that mysterious faculty that guided my hand, the one that always helped me decide where to put the next brushstroke. This wasn't an "ought" or a "should"; it was a deep sense of rightness, and of pleasure in rightness. I began applying this to the rest of life, and slowly my physical state improved; I had much more energy. I found that I was actually accomplishing more, retaining more of my studies, experiencing deeper, more sincere prayer, more focused meditation. And now it felt like mine.

• • •

AFTER I'D SPENT ALMOST seven years in yeshiva, it was time to consider my next steps. I knew I wanted to teach, find a way to continue to study, and integrate the things that mattered most to me: religious thought, education, and art. At the same time, I wanted a life that was sane, grounded. I wanted to bring all that I had learned, all I'd experienced, into the "real world" I'd left behind. Our third child, another boy, was born. Suddenly outnumbered by our children, my wife and I also realized we needed to make some real income if we were going to successfully run a household.

My teachers had encouraged, cajoled, and pressured me to become a rabbi. I felt, after so many years of study supported by family and scholarships, that I had a lot to pay forward. But becoming a pulpit rabbi didn't feel right. During a brief summer trip to the States, I went to see Professor Wiesel at his New York home for advice.

He listened intently to my question and replied, "My teacher Saul Lieberman taught at the seminary for many years. Many of his students became rabbis. When they asked him about rabbinic positions in synagogues, he always used to reply, 'A *pulpit?* You want to take a *pulpit?*' He hated the idea of his students becoming synagogue rabbis. There is a lot of pressure, you work for your synagogue's board, and often there isn't a lot of time to teach."

Then he said, "Why don't you come to Boston University, and you can be my teaching assistant? My current assistants are graduating, so I have an opening. I will help you enroll in the doctoral program there. I told you that I would wait for you."

I was surprised and I told him so. He smiled broadly and said, "Ariel, did you think I was being polite? I meant it."

I accepted on the spot.

My yeshiva teachers spent the next weeks trying to get me to reconsider, hoping I would take a more traditional rabbinic path, but I refused. When they saw that I wouldn't be swayed, they gave me their blessing, along with the rabbinic ordination I'd been working toward all those years.

Weeks later, I arrived in New York with Sabrina and three small children, all of us exhausted from the eleven-hour flight from Israel. Young and inexperienced parents that we were, we'd given the two older kids chocolate on the plane, hoping it would settle them, but of course it did the opposite, and they hardly slept. Even when we arrived at my father's house in Queens, the three of them wouldn't close their eyes. Sabrina and I spent over an hour walking them in their strollers, taking turns wearing the baby in a carrier, hoping the gentle motion would lull them to sleep. We walked and cried with weariness. Welcome home.

In addition to all the logistics of packing up, booking flights, and finding a new place to live—not to mention buying new clothes (at the time I owned only a handful of shirts and a few pairs of black pants)—I had to reorient myself to the world after years of living on a literal and figurative mountaintop. My anchor was Professor Wiesel, the person with whom I'd shared my deepest, most personal questions. I sensed that the golden light of mysticism wasn't foreign to him but that he was able to integrate—with grace and seeming ease—thought and action, spirituality and worldliness. I knew I needed to find a ladder with which I could descend back to earth, and I knew he could help me.

I needed time for reflection, but there wasn't any time because school was starting. In an early meeting, I shared my feelings of disorientation with him, explained how difficult I found it to suddenly be in the noisy city, to be starting an American PhD program after years of living in an isolated outpost.

He smiled and said, "You were in yeshiva, and now you will continue to learn with me. It's good, and it won't be as different as you think." Then he added, "When I was young, I thought I would live in the world of the yeshiva for my whole life. But you can bring the yeshiva to the university. You can study the same texts, but with greater diversity of perspective. You can create space for the same kind of reflection about the same questions you had there. Who says God cannot speak to you in the university?"

The immensity of my relief at this moment robbed me of my voice. Casting about for something to say to cover my emotion, I told him that I was nervous about talking to large classes as his teaching assistant.

He nodded. "To this day, whenever I give a lecture, as I walk out onto the stage I think to myself, *Why am I doing this?* When I walk off the stage afterward I think, *Why did I do that?*"

We laughed, and instantly I felt better, ready to begin. I thought to myself, *The golden light is here too. It's in laughter that we are holy.*

5
Activism

I would have given all the prizes, all the honors, for one life,
even one life that would not have been taken away.

— ELIE WIESEL

"Hatred Is a Kind of Insanity"

"J. ROBERT OPPENHEIMER, the Nobel Prize–nominated father of the atom bomb, once testified before a congressional committee on nuclear power and its dangers. After hearing his testimony, a congressman asked him how the U.S. could avoid nuclear war. Oppenheimer simply said, 'Make peace, sir.'"

It is halfway through my first semester as Professor Wiesel's teaching assistant, and our readings and discussions on the theme of faith and power have led us to this lecture on the history of violence. Professor Wiesel had begun the semester focusing on each reading—Ariel Dorfman's *Death and the Maiden*, Toni Morrison's *Sula*, Ismail Kadare's *Elegy for Kosovo*, and Vasily Grossman's *Life and Fate*—but now he employed a wider lens, turning to a broad examination of the origins of war and drawing on the books we have read as a class.

I'm just starting to feel comfortable with the rhythm of lectures, discussion sections, office hours, and my own course work. Only a few months ago I was still in Israel, in yeshiva, living in a situation fraught with conflict. I still expect to hear news of bombings, shootings, and stone-throwing incidents on the radio. Here in Boston, everything is calm, sunny, relaxed. But maybe because of this lecture's topic, I feel more tense than I have since arriving.

Professor Wiesel goes on: "Just like that. It sounds so simple. And yet it is not simple — why not? We have so many questions. What makes one human being kill another? What makes a person choose inhumanity to affirm his humanity? Hatred is a kind of insanity. It serves no purpose, does not build anything, it only destroys. What are its underlying causes? What elements in human psychology lead to violence? And how, really, how can anyone choose to take a life?"

Professor Wiesel's preoccupation with the problem of hatred was urgent due to his fierce commitment to ensure that his own experience of suffering and abandonment would not be repeated. This urgency translated into recurring trips to conflict zones. Starting in the 1950s as a journalist and later as a writer and witness, he traveled to hot spots around the globe — Nicaragua, Cambodia, South Africa, Bosnia, to name just a few.

I had seen the images of him wearing a flak jacket and slightly too-large helmet that appeared in newspapers after his 1992 tour of Bosnia. The memory of our soft-spoken professor in military camouflage brought home for me the sincerity of his belief that discussions were not enough, that the test of an idea, no matter how compelling, was the extent to which it compelled action on behalf of others. He worked hard to transmit this belief to his students so that the project of ending hatred, the work of many lifetimes, would continue. He once told his class, "Teaching for me is a sharing of determination, that mine will become a part of *your* determination, so that you will continue doing good things after I am gone." Many students in his classes went on to become activists, and the ways in which they did so were myriad and sometimes surprising.

Now, in class, a journalism graduate student named Valery raises her hand, and Professor Wiesel nods to her. "After all your work, and all your thinking about this . . . if we really want to transform hate, where do we start?"

He opens his hands like a supplicant and replies, "If I knew . . . I have spent many years asking that question. Hatred is like a cancer, and it transcends all boundaries—religious, ethnic, national. It is contagious, spreading from one person or community to another, always ending in more hatred and destruction. When I brought together thinkers and activists to explore issues confronting humanity, I called the conferences the Anatomy of Hate, because we were trying to understand the sources of human hatred and how to respond to it. One thing we have learned: When you face evil, don't let it grow, fight it right away. Had Hitler been fought immediately there would have been no Holocaust. Be watchful.

"To be human is to share a common origin. And if we share a common origin, our destinies are entwined. What happens to me will eventually happen to you; what happened to my people is a foreshadowing of what will threaten the world. Auschwitz led to Hiroshima and who knows what else? Therefore the most important biblical commandment is *Lo taamod al dam réakha*, 'Thou shall not stand idly by the shedding of the blood of thy fellow human being.' The word *réakha*, 'fellow human being'—it is universal. *Anyone* who is suffering, *anyone* who is threatened becomes your responsibility. If you can feel this and act with even a little bit more humanity, more sensitivity, as a result, that is the beginning. It is not the end—I do not know how to end hatred, I truly wish I did—but recognizing our shared humanity is a good beginning."

AFTER CLASS, I KNOCK on Professor Wiesel's door. He greets me, finishes signing a letter, and puts it neatly into a pile. I notice a stack of books on his desk, books he has assigned for our courses—the Bhagavad Gita, works by Euripides, Brecht, Kafka. He walks over to the little seating area by the bay windows and gestures for me to join him so we can discuss my doctoral dissertation.

I tell him that recently, when I was visiting my grandparents in Florida, I woke up in the middle of the night with an idea for my thesis. I would examine nonviolence in Hasidic sources through a case study of sectarian conflict between two Hasidic groups in 1830s Ukraine. I got out of bed, walked over to the table in the guest room of my grandparents' house, wrote down some ideas and some questions, and went back to bed. But I couldn't sleep. My mind was racing, filled with texts that seemed relevant to this project. I got up again, walked over to the table, wrote down a list of sources to review, then went to bed again. Again, I could not sleep; questions roiled my mind, imaginary conversations between mystics and civil rights leaders. I was awake for most of that night asking questions: What would Martin Luther King Jr. have said to the Hasidim who were being persecuted by another, more powerful sect? How did the weaker group's leader persuade his young disciples not to respond with aggression to their antagonists? What is the relationship between religious practices and peacemaking in Jewish sources?

Professor Wiesel says, "Ariel, this is good. Revealing the connections between religious literature, especially lesser-known texts, and practical application is important. You should focus on the specific period you're most interested in rather than including a survey of Jewish teachings on peace and peacemaking—that's too broad. But this example will help reveal both the dynamics of and a religious response to conflict."

Then he asks me a personal question. "I want to know one thing. What in this topic is important to *you*?"

I think for a moment, then tell him that I have always been fascinated by peacemakers. Whether it was reconciling the two homes I grew up in, participating in interreligious dialogue between people hurt in the Middle East conflict, or simply my own internal wrestling with competing values, one question I consistently saw at the heart of my life was *How do we make peace?*

"But it's not a simple question for me," I tell Professor Wiesel.

"Why is that?"

I say, "When I was in Israel, I saw two very different kinds of peacemaking work. The first was when modern, Western groups tried to impose a modern narrative on local communities, to tell both Israeli Jews and Palestinian Muslims that compromise, universal rights, and moderate policies were in everyone's best economic and political interests. This was the approach of Oslo and other peace accords, the method of politicians.

"The second approach was more organic. It appealed to the sources of meaning and religious texts of local communities, using the language of prayer and sacred stories to inspire change. It seems to me that this approach worked better and had more staying power, because it appealed directly to people's worldview, their sense of faith and meaning. Because my project is partly inspired by encounters with these kinds of peacemakers, I am sensitive to the first, top-down approach. And this approach defines a lot of the literature of conflict transformation. Some of that literature is very self-righteous; it represents an attitude of poor listening, and it doesn't inspire local religious actors to find their way to peace. That's why I want to explore *religious* sources of conflict transformation."

Professor Wiesel replies, "Well, really, any sincere attempt to make peace is good and should be supported. But it is true, it is very important when engaging in peacemaking, or any activism, really, to question yourself, to question your assumptions, to be precise with language, and, especially, to listen. I have spent a lot of time at the United Nations, where some of the worst violators of human rights sit on the Human Rights Council. I have seen the conflation and facile comparisons of morally different situations. And who has not heard a celebrity discussing people's suffering only to enhance his own image? It is important, and it is possible to break through those distortions. But you must study — conflict resolution, yes, but also human rights and its history, as well as specific examples of its application. That way you will know how it has been used as a weapon and also how it has solved real problems."

"How Would I Live with Myself?"

THE NEXT WEEK IN LECTURE, Professor Wiesel asks students to share their questions about the readings or about the issues raised in class so far. The first comes from Dave, a tall undergrad with thick glasses and long blond dreadlocks. "Professor, how did you first get involved in human rights activism?"

"Well, you know I was a journalist for many years, in France and then in the United States. I worked for a Yiddish newspaper, then for an Israeli one, and I was paid a few pennies per article. The main advantage was that they sent me to many places I otherwise would not have visited. And I saw suffering in many places. I learned of conflicts, acts of oppression and inhumanity, around the world. The poor in India, the boat people of Vietnam, the victims of the Khmer Rouge in Cambodia, the Mesquite Indians in South America. And knowing what I know, seeing what I have seen, how could I not do something, anything, to help? But what could I do? I was a poor journalist, a writer. So I wrote about it, in articles, interviews, and, later, some essays in my books. Even later, I wrote op-eds in the *New York Times* and elsewhere when a response was needed. I also started gathering others, Nobel Prize winners, writers, anyone with any influence who wanted to help. I used words to try to change facts, to create new realities."

"Do words really help, though?" Dave asks.

"They are all we have sometimes. If they are words of testimony, if they are not abstractions, merely ideas, they have a certain power. That is why I felt, even after I was no longer a journalist, that I must travel to those places to see what was happening for myself. I knew that if I could bear witness with my own eyes, I would have a chance of conveying what I have seen with authenticity, and therefore with power."

Valery, the journalism student, raises her hand and asks, "Was writing about other people's suffering similar to writing about your own?"

"It is similar, and it is different. When I went to Cambodia or Bosnia, my experience allowed me to see theirs with more compassion and perhaps with greater understanding. Almost as if, having lived through one catastrophe, I could bear witness to others more deeply. One thing emerged from the other—my attempts to change things, to fight indifference, emerged directly from my own experience."

"Did you find it easy, being an activist?" asks a French exchange student named Colleen.

"Oh no. I am very shy, believe me. It is not easy for me to speak up, to be on camera. But I could not be silent. How would I live with myself?"

Valery asks, "Can anyone do this? Does anyone have the authority to be an activist?"

Professor Wiesel replies, "Moral authority doesn't develop spontaneously; it must be earned. Arthur Koestler, whose book *Darkness at Noon* we have read, once asked, 'Can a conscience function by proxy?' The answer is no, it cannot. You must take action yourself, even if it is a small, modest action. You cannot pass it off to someone else. You build the authority by doing it; you do not wait for someone to give you permission."

Professor Wiesel's own authority followed this pattern. As a Holocaust survivor, as the author of *Night,* he certainly had the authority of suffering, of survival, early in his career. But it was by standing in solidarity with other oppressed people, by visiting conflict zones in person, that his authority gained real influence. It was the act of bearing witness to suffering, not public posturing or armchair commentary, that gave him the moral weight to "speak truth to power." He showed up, again and again, with the only tools he had: his eyes, his heart, and his words. Until he was awarded the Nobel Peace Prize in 1986, he was an independent scholar-author-activist, representing no organization, agency, or constituency. After the Nobel, when he established the Elie Wiesel Foundation for Humanity, he had a larger platform, and that enabled him to purchase ad space in major newspapers and convene meetings of Nobel laureates. But he never lost the commitment to acting independently with total freedom and autonomy. He often spoke of this, noting that even when he was speaking in the White House or at the United Nations, he felt like a yeshiva *bachur* (a student) from a little town, a member of no group or committee, armed only with words.

In October 2006, Professor Wiesel took me aside after class to tell me that he had been offered the position of president of the state of Israel and that he had declined. The presidency, a post also offered to Albert Einstein in 1952, is a largely symbolic and diplomatic position. Its holder does not have to attend parliamentary meetings or get involved in the often aggravating work of parliamentary coalition politics.

"You said no? But why?" I asked.

"I have never spoken for anyone but myself; I would not want my words to be used as a political tool, even for the Jewish state, which I love."

"But you could do so much good with a platform like that!"
"I'm a teacher and a writer, not a politician."

From Sarajevo to Sarajevo

NEXT WEEK IN CLASS, Professor Wiesel returns to Dave's
question. "You asked whether words are enough. Sometimes
they are not. When it came to Bosnia, with a heavy heart I
supported the U.S. and NATO decision to go to war, in order
to stop the mass rape, murders, and deportations. Otherwise
how can I complain of the world's silence in my time? I don't
want people to ask *our* generation, Why were you silent? We
cannot allow the killers to get away with it. It is intolerable,
wherever it happens. So we speak, we write, but when innocent people are dying, sometimes we must also act.

"I was in Sarajevo in the early 1990s, and I cannot forget. I
spent four days on a mission to see what was happening, and
I left with more questions than when I arrived. I saw a city
in ruins, people cold and starving, displaced . . . The cold was
very bad; temperatures reached thirty or forty degrees below zero, and people would collect wood, newspaper, anything that would burn, from beneath the snow. The silence
was punctuated by occasional shooting, and stray bullets
were a danger throughout the city. I saw the ashes of thousands of books; the national library had been burned a few
months earlier. And I met with Izetbegovic, who was president of Bosnia-Herzegovina and the leader of the Muslims,
and Karadzic, who at that point had occupied most of Bos-

nia. I begged them to sit down with one another, to speak, so that no more children would be killed. But neither would sit with the other. The Muslims felt unable to speak to the Serbian perpetrators of so many killings. The Serbians accused their victims of lying, of exaggerating their losses. It was very demoralizing."

"Were you afraid?" asks Valery.

"It was dangerous. At one point, one of our group said that he was nervous because we were near an area called Sniper's Alley, so we moved away. But in general, I did not feel afraid. I felt frustration, because all of this bloodshed was so *stupid!*" He slices the air with his hand as he says this word. "And children were dying because of the stupidity and hatred of adults.

"I also felt frustration because the leaders tried to manipulate me several times. Before I went there, I made them promise that there would be no state dinners, no formal receptions of any kind. I was there as a private person; I didn't represent any organization. A dinner would make it look like I was adding credibility to their government, which was not my intention at all. At one point, the president took me by the arm and led me through a door. I thought we were going outside, but suddenly, I found myself at a state dinner! There were officials, journalists. It was exactly what I had said I would not do. I asked for everyone's attention, and I told them, 'It is Friday evening, and the place of a Jew on Friday evening is the synagogue.' And I left. I would not allow myself to become a prop for someone else's agenda, especially not there, where every gesture was scrutinized and interpreted by the different sides."

"Did anything good come from that trip?" asked Thomas, a grad student in international relations.

"Well, I was able to bring Bosnia to the attention of the U.S. government, President Clinton, and others, and this played some part in the American and NATO decision to intervene. And, perhaps, the shame the world felt at allowing another atrocity to occur led to the creation of the international tribunal for the former Yugoslavia, which indicted many people."

It was Wiesel's public testimony about his visit to Sarajevo that persuaded President Clinton to intervene.

"What's it like, meeting the president?" asks Valery.

He answers with a mischievous smile. "It makes me hungry. When I visit the White House I don't eat. Why? Because when the president speaks, I cannot eat. And when he is silent, *I* am speaking. So I leave the White House hungry every time." He chuckles, then becomes serious again.

"But while there was an intervention, the siege of Sarajevo lasted almost four years—longer than the siege of Leningrad; it was the longest siege of a city in modern times. A siege is a war against civilians. The history of such tragedies is filled with stories of belated accountability—the world, if it acts at all, acts too late. This is the definition of tragedy: too late. So, yes, some positive things happened. But they cannot bring back the dead or heal the wounded.

"I have often thought since then that the twentieth century can be described as a tragic journey from Sarajevo to Sarajevo. It began in that city with the assassination of Archduke Franz Ferdinand, which led to millions of deaths during the First World War, the end of several empires, and new national boundaries. And it ended in that same place, with mass murder."

Why Did Cain Kill Abel?

THE FOLLOWING WEEK Professor Wiesel brings the discussion back to literature. "As always, if we want to understand what is happening today, we must look to the past. To try to understand the roots of hatred, we can look at our earliest sources of wisdom. It begins in the Bible, with the first killing, a brother killing his brother. Half of humanity killed the other half. One half of humanity became killer, the other half, victim.

"Why did Cain kill Abel? The verse tells us that, just before the act, Cain spoke to Abel. But it does not tell us what he said. It says, literally, 'And Cain said to Abel' — period. It does not tell us the content of his words. Why is that?"

After a moment, a student named Emily says, "Maybe the Bible doesn't report what he said because it's not important. Things between them had reached a point where no message could have helped."

"Good," Professor Wiesel says. "Which means that there was no communication, actually, and that was the problem. When language fails, when there is no communication, the result is violence.

"But there are many other reasons for the violence offered by the commentators: Cain was jealous of his brother, whose sacrifice, unlike his own, was accepted by God. Or they fought over who they would each marry, Cain wanting both his own twin sister and Abel's as wives. Or they fought over territory, or over competing ways of life, agricultural versus hunter-gatherer. There are many commentaries, many theories, but in the end there was death.

"And what happens next? God tells Cain, 'Your brother's *bloods* cry out to me from the earth.' *Bloods*, plural. And all the commentators remark: Cain did not only murder his brother, he erased all the descendants that would have come from him. He canceled their existence. And this is true with every life lost. Think of how many children the six million would have had, how many grandchildren, great-grandchildren. Think of the victims in Cambodia, in Rwanda, in Darfur, the generations that will not be born. And think that among them may have been one who would have found a cure for cancer, or diabetes, or Alzheimer's. How many great philosophers, great writers and artists, great peacemakers, were lost? When the killer kills, he harms himself and all of humanity too."

Valery jumps in. "In this story, it sounds like hatred and murder are inherent parts of us. Cain wasn't even part of a culture, right? I mean, he didn't go to school and fall in with the wrong crowd. He just hated."

"Right," says Professor Wiesel. "Although you must remember that other things have happened already in the story, other traumas — the exile from the Garden of Eden, its effect on Adam and Eve. What kind of parents were they? Were they attentive to their children? Did they play favorites? In literature, as in life, we must try to understand, to trace the roots of violence. At the same time, it remains mysterious. Many killers, including those who perpetrated the September 11 attacks, came from wealthy homes and were educated. Though no explanation can justify violence, still we seek to understand.

"We must look at the line drawn between self and other, friend and stranger. Is this an essential part of our nature, as some psychologists argue? Is it a learned behavior? The idea of an in-group that is opposed to outsiders, the rise of tribalism and then of triumphalism, is a critical thread in human history. For me to feel strong and confident, I must belittle you — this is one cause of bullying among children. For one group to feel special, chosen, destined, we must denigrate *other* groups — this has led to oppression, religious wars, and other forms of conflict.

"In my tradition, triumphalism and holiness are opposing principles. We should be the brother, not the master, of somebody else. There is a famous teaching that appears in the biblical discussion of the laws of kosher food. Many birds are not kosher — we are not allowed to eat eagles, vultures, birds of prey. But there is one, the stork, that is not kosher even though it is not a bird of prey and even though its name in Hebrew, *hasidah*, means 'the kind one.' The commentators ask, Why is it not kosher? The answer: True, it is a creature known for its kindness. But it is generous only with its own species; to others, it is cruel. Therefore it is not kosher, to teach us not to be like that. Kindness and compassion must not end with your own community."

War and Peace, Life and Fate

"I THINK OF THE murderers, and I am filled with despair. I think of the victims, and I am filled with love. I think of the Jewish children murdered in my time. If from now until I die I were to do nothing but name them, simply recite name after name, I would die before reaching the end of the list. And we must at least remember their names. So many of them have no graves."

Professor Wiesel continues. "Sometimes you feel that history is blushing. War has its own logic, its own language, its own laws. In times of war, especially when civilians are affected, mothers are afraid to send their children to school; friends wonder if friends will come back from a café or restaurant. From the vantage point of peace, it is insane. There is a famous story from Greek literature concerning a king named Perus and his adviser Kinias. King Perus is bored, so bored, and he tells Kinias, his adviser, that in order to relieve his boredom, he will make war and then return home. Kinias, a wise man, says, 'Why not just stay home?' What is the point of war, after all? So there will be more lives ended, more orphans, and more tears?

"We have seen this in the literature we have studied together. In *Life and Fate* by Vasily Grossman, one of my very favorite works of literature, we encounter the deaths of three hundred and fifty thousand people at Stalingrad at the end of World War Two. The author attempts to humanize the vast scope of this battle through very small details: a mother's tears as her son goes to the war, a daughter-in-law's refusal to bring her husband's mother into their home and the subsequent murder of the mother by the Nazis, the concern over rations among soldiers at the front. You must decide whether he succeeded, whether the Battle of Stalingrad has become a human event for you."

Dave pushes his dreadlocks away from his face and raises his hand. "The book is so long and so dense that at first I found it overwhelming. But I was drawn in by the details you're talking about, and by about halfway through I couldn't put it down—

though I still needed to look at the index of names, the long Russian names, to keep track of some of the characters. But it made me think that maybe the way to deal with other big issues in our world, whether we're talking about war or hunger or other things, is to focus in on specific stories." I see several students nodding in agreement.

"You are right," says Professor Wiesel. "You know, the details Grossman shows us come from his experience. He participated in the war, as a reporter at the front. The Siege of Stalingrad lasted over five months, from autumn of 1942 until winter of 1943. There was starvation, cannibalism . . . a single air raid of six hundred planes killed forty thousand civilians! So it is difficult to truly convey the experience — it was so absurdly destructive. It is also morally difficult because it was a clash of two dictatorships, Communist and fascist. Both agreed that the ends justified the means. The difference was that Germany oppressed the other, the nations and peoples it conquered. Russia oppressed its own people. That's why in Germany there was internal resistance, while under Stalin there was not. The oppression was too paralyzing — the fear of being informed on by friends, neighbors, even family. Grossman himself was the victim of such a betrayal; his editor informed on him to the secret police. His manuscript was confiscated — even the typewriter ribbon upon which he wrote it was taken! — and he died without seeing the novel published. Even his *name* was forbidden by the Soviet authorities; it was illegal to mention his name in print for twenty years. So Grossman drew on his immediate experiences to humanize what could have been an abstract portrait of the war.

"Grossman believed, and he shows us, that Communism

and Nazism are two sides of the same coin. Both suppress dissent, both destroy freedom and individuality, both carefully and deliberately place boot heels on the throats of human beings. Grossman has Liss, the Gestapo officer, tell Mostovskoy, the old Bolshevik official, 'When we look one another in the face, we're neither of us just looking at a face we hate—no, we're gazing into a mirror. That's the tragedy of our age.'

"And yet Grossman was an optimist and argued for the triumph of humanity over war. One of the strongest moments in the novel is the encounter between a German soldier and a Russian soldier in the no man's land between the lines. It takes place just after a terrible bombardment, with the unendurable noise of explosions, and dust and bricks falling into the foxhole where they cower. Klimov, the Russian soldier, encouraged himself during the bombing by squeezing the hand of his comrade. But when the dust settles, he discovers that he has been holding the hand of the enemy, a German soldier. Grossman writes, 'They looked at each other in silence, two inhabitants of the war. The perfect, faultless, automatic reflex they both possessed—the instinct to kill—failed to function.' This is one of my favorite lines in literature. The soldiers walked away to their respective armies, perhaps to fight or kill another day. But for that moment, humanity prevailed.

"As you said, Dave, our success in responding to worldchanging events is often measured by the small moments and encounters. If we can act with greater sensitivity to others, if we act with courage and choose humanity over inhumanity, it does not seem that it can affect the larger trajectory of history. But I believe it can."

• • •

A WEEK LATER, in a lecture on the Greek tragedian Euripides, Professor Wiesel says, "I am trying to teach you beauty. We need to remember that doing good and making peace are not only right, they are beautiful acts. I was in a bunker in Israel during the first Iraq war, in 1991. Missiles sent by Saddam Hussein were falling in major cities, and families were spending a lot of time in bomb shelters. Even children had to have gas masks ready in case of an attack. During one of the raids, I sat next to an old woman who seemed terrified. We could hear the sirens, and the radio reporting where the missiles were falling. At one point, I touched her arm and said, 'What a world, eh?' And she said, 'Oh my, yes, what a filthy world.' War is an ethical problem. But it is also an aesthetic problem.

"Euripides was a deeply political author who tried to show the ugliness of war. Most of his works were written during time of war. His play *Medea* has no heroes, and it is meant as a warning of what happens when civility breaks down and is replaced by anger and the lust for revenge. The play must have been shocking to its original audience. Medea has murdered her own two young sons in an act of revenge, but then she is taken into the sky by Helios, charioteer of the sun, who usually represents nobility, purity. Morality has been turned on its head. Euripides is commenting on the war of his time, showing its effects on civilization.

"Euripides's *Trojan Women* shows us the aftermath of the Trojan War and its ugliness. It is through the eyes of women that he shows us this perspective, through the victims who have been taken from home, whose husbands and sons have been killed. Here we have the victims' pathetic voices." He reads:

We stand at the same point of pain.
We too are slaves.
Our children are crying, calling to us with tears, "Mother, I am
    all alone.
To the dark ships now they drive me,
And I cannot see you, Mother."

Professor Wiesel continues: "Later, Euripides has Astyanax, a young boy, condemned to death by the victorious Greeks. 'Behold, hapless women of Troy, the corpse of Astyanax! Whom the Danai have cruelly slain by throwing him from the battlements.' Why? Because he is the son of Hector, and the victors are concerned that he will grow up to avenge his father's death. Again we see how war leads to more death. But he is merely a boy, guilty only of a possible future act. And his mother witnesses all this . . . it is ugly, as war is ugly. And a work of art that shows the ugliness of war is more beautiful, because it is true, than one which romanticizes it.

"Euripides and the Bible have something in common here. Both the Greek and the Hebrew tradition are replete with violence, and both contain strong antiwar messages. For example, when the children of Israel are saved from the Egyptian armies, which are drowned in the Red Sea, there is a legend that God commands the angels not to sing, saying, 'My creatures are drowning and you sing?' The victims can sing for their own salvation; the angels, who are merely bystanders, cannot. And remember, the book of Joshua, which is a book of war, has no song in it. Where there is war, there cannot be poetry.

"In the Bible's discussion of war, we find a moment of sensitivity. In Deuteronomy it is written that the leaders speak to the assembled army, and they say the following. 'He who has built a house, or planted a vineyard, or recently gotten married, or one who is afraid of war, fearful . . . can go home.' Just like that. And the commentaries say, 'Look how careful the law is to not humiliate a coward. In order that he should not be embarrassed in public, we put him together with the others, with other reasons to leave the battlefield, so that no one will know who is leaving because he just married and who is leaving because he is afraid.' And, of course, on a practical level, this opens the way for conscientious objectors as well.

"David, whose life was driven by a vision of an ideal city, Jerusalem, was not allowed by God to build the Temple. After all his yearning to do so — the psalmist speaks of this yearning — why was he unable to fulfill his dearest wish? Because his hands were red with blood. He fought too many wars. David was following God's orders, but if you have shed blood, you cannot build the temple of God. In fact, when David's son Solomon built the Temple later, he was not even allowed to use iron tools to build it, because of their association with war.

"There is a legend about this, how Solomon didn't know what to do — how will he cut the stones to build the temple without using metal instruments? Until he heard of a strange creature called the *shamir,* a kind of worm that eats through stone. The legend describes his quest for this worm and how he tricked the king of demons to help him find it and how he used it to build the Temple in Jerusalem. But the basic message is this: The meeting place of God and man must be completely free of the stain of violence. Violence and all good things — spirituality, nobility, beauty — are mutually exclusive.

"Strangely, soldiers are the ones who know this best. It is difficult to romanticize violence when you have seen it yourself. Soldiers often become peacemakers; they are the ones who despise war the most. I remember, I once asked Yitzhak Rabin, the general who was responsible for Israel's extraordinary victory in 1967 against much greater forces, 'Why was there no victory parade after the war?' Rabin told me, 'It is because our soldiers were sad. They were sad for their own losses, of course. But they were also sad for the enemy's losses.' They did not romanticize or celebrate the war. Even in a situation of defensive war, this is a very human attitude.

"Some stories begin with bloodshed. Others, like *Romeo and Juliet,* which we studied a few weeks ago, begin with love and end with bloodshed. *Romeo and Juliet* is not a love story. They did not die because they loved each other; they died because their parents hated each other. Why? Because of a feud, the echoes of an injury done generations ago. I saw the same thing in Bosnia, a place where blood feuds caused people to kill each other, eventually leading to mass murder. And why? Because of something one person's great-grandfather did to another's decades ago. Sometimes they could not even remember what the original problem was! They just knew they hated one another . . . I think this is why Shakespeare does not tell us the reason for the feud between the Montagues and Capulets—because they themselves have forgotten the reason. He only shows us its effects: the deaths of two young people who loved each other and the erasure of their future children."

"Is the tragedy the parents' fault, then? Is hatred learned from parents?" asks Julie, a postdoc in psychology.

"Hatred can be transmitted by parents. We have seen chil-

dren who were victims, but we have also seen children who became killers. School shootings, Columbine and elsewhere . . .
the Columbine shooters were fascinated by Hitler. He is dead,
but in a way, he is still killing people. Do they learn this from
adults? Are they given permission to release the hate that is already there?

"The first time I went to Cambodia, I visited a refugee camp
near Aranyaprathet. At one point, one of the guides took me
aside, pointed, and said, 'Do you see that barracks?' Inside
there were some eight hundred children, twelve-, thirteen-,
and fourteen-year-olds. They were kept always separate, they
ate separately, went outside only when the yard was empty of
other prisoners. These children were soldiers of the Khmer
Rouge; they were among the killers responsible for the Cambodian genocide. The Khmer Rouge believed that they could
erase all of human history, bring history back to zero and begin again, and they used *children* as tools in this campaign.
What happened? How did that society turn children into murderers of their own parents and friends? Somehow, hatred was
contagious, was transmitted through a horrific education, and
this was powerful enough to overwhelm their basic sense of
humanity.

"But the opposite can also be taught. The presence of elders can make a difference. In my little town, and in communities all over before the war, we did not send old people away.
Grandparents lived with the family; the generations were together. Now we send old people to Florida, to retirement communities, where we do not need to see them. As a result, memories are not transmitted. It is the elders who remember war
and its costs, who bear the stories that shape children as re-

sponsible people, members of a community. In their absence, it may be easier for hatred to grow."

Real Time: Darfur

THE GENOCIDE IN DARFUR, in Western Sudan, began in 2003. News reports emerged of attacks by the Janjaweed, which means "killers on horseback" in Arabic, on innocent non-Arab men, women, and children. Mass rapes, mass graves. This was genocide redux; as early as the 1990s, attacks against non-Arabs had taken place. Wiesel was quoted describing those earlier killings in Southern Sudan as "genocide in slow motion." His public statements echoed things he said to us in class. He told us he was working behind the scenes to persuade officials to intervene. He wrote op-eds in the *New York Times,* some of them signed by a long list of Nobel laureates.

In lecture, students asked him for more information about the reports. Because the government of Omar Hassan al-Bashir claimed that what was happening was civil war and not genocide, some students were confused. Which is it? they asked. How do we distinguish genocide from other categories of atrocity?

"First," said Professor Wiesel, "I hope you feel, as I do, the sadness of having so many categories, so many names, for violence. I wish we had only to use language to describe good things, varieties of a child's smile, modalities of friendship. But in answer to your question, what is happening in Darfur *is* genocide. It is a deliberate attempt to destroy ethnic groups, one that has already led to so many deaths, so many people displaced, and hungry. I am working now to persuade the U.S. State Department to call what is happening a genocide."

Dave asked, "Why does it matter what we call it? Does it really make that much of a difference?"

"Language is very important. Just as it can electrify groups, spurring them to violence, it can also catalyze a response in the international community. If we call this genocide, it will be more difficult for the international community to avoid action. But we must be careful too — not everything is genocide. The UN Genocide Convention defines *genocide* as 'the specific intent to destroy a national, ethnic, racial, or religious group.' It is often difficult to prove such intent. There are situations that are mass murder, and that is enough — we do not need to use the language of genocide to spur action. But if it is genocide, and what is happening in Darfur is, we must call it by its name. I am working on this now."

The following year, in September 2004, the UN Security Council drafted Resolution 1564, which named the atrocities in Darfur genocide, called on the United Nations and its members, particularly in African and Arab nations, to take action to stop it, and called on the U.S. administration to adopt the genocide label as well. Two days later, U.S. secretary of state Colin Powell publicly did so, testifying before a Senate committee that the Sudanese campaign against non-Arabs was genocide. This was the first time the executive branch of the U.S. government used that term to describe a current conflict. But this label did not lead to concerted intervention by other nations, though it did lead to the Save Darfur campaign, which was spurred by the genocide label and initially spearheaded by the United States Holocaust Museum in Washington and the American Jewish World Service. Soon thereafter, many other organizations joined in and succeeded in raising awareness and humanitarian aid for displaced victims.

In October 2004, Professor Wiesel told us of his meeting with the UN secretary-general just a few days earlier. "I met with Kofi Annan to push for more action on Darfur. I asked him to publish a daily death toll in Darfur, one that would be shared around the world. It would make it more difficult to look away." But he remained skeptical that meaningful action would take place. "We have had such discussions before. There is political resistance, inertia, fear of entanglement or escalation." He leaned forward and said, "But it is a scandal that we have not stopped the bloodshed in Darfur. It is insulting to the victims, and to our own past, that we do not act! Where is the outcry?

"What I would really like to see is leaders who are responsible for mass murder tried before the International Criminal Court. First, maybe it will cause others to hesitate, to know there will be consequences. And second, even if that is not the case, at least it may awaken the rest of the world."

As he spoke, I could feel his urgency. Later, he told me that when he said in class that he could not sleep because people somewhere were suffering, he meant it literally—he suffered from insomnia.

Once, when he spoke of this urgency, a student named Dana asked him what role the Nobel Peace Prize had played in his life, whether it helped him have a greater impact. Professor Wiesel said, "I would have given all the prizes, all the honors, for one life, even one life that would not have been taken away."

By 2009, the death toll in Darfur had risen to three hundred thousand, and more than two and a half million people were displaced. Jewish and Armenian groups were especially galvanized by the use of the term *genocide* to describe the events in Bosnia, and their activities and others' reached a tipping point. That year, President al-Bashir was indicted by the International Criminal Court for his role in masterminding the atrocities in Darfur. He was the first sitting president to be so indicted. But he was never arrested, and reports of atrocities, including the use of chemical weapons against civilians, continued.

"I Felt My Future Changing"

TOWARD THE END OF the semester, my first as Professor Wiesel's TA, Dave comes to see me again. He sits down, pulls his dreadlocks back into a loose ponytail, clears his throat, and says, "I want to talk about a decision I need to make."

He looks serious, preoccupied. "I don't know if I told you that I've been working as a park ranger for the past few summers. It doesn't pay that well, but I love the quiet, being in nature . . . it gives me time to think. I was going to do that fulltime, make a career of it. I've done a lot of research and I had a plan in place. But now it doesn't feel right anymore."

"What do you mean?" I ask.

"Well, after taking this class and hearing Professor Wiesel talk about his life and what he's done to try to help people . . . I don't think I can spend my life alone in the woods. I think I have to do something that will help too. I'm seriously considering becoming a priest."

"A priest?" I repeat. "Is this something you've thought about before?"

"Yes, sort of. I have an uncle who's a priest. But he's a parish priest in England. I'm thinking about a different kind of ministry, working with homeless people in my hometown, Chicago."

"That's amazing, and it's important work," I say. "But it's as far as you can get from being a park ranger. Don't you need the nature too, for your own well-being?"

"I do, I do. I'm thinking I can spend summers in one of the national parks, either as a ranger or just on my own, hiking and camping, to refuel. But homelessness is really an urban issue, and I feel called to it. When Professor Wiesel talked about the small moments making a big difference, it hit me very deeply. I told you once that I feel I'm betraying what I've learned by not practicing it. Now I'll get to practice it."

AS OF THIS WRITING, Dave is a priest in downtown Chicago, ministering to the homeless. He still spends some weekends hiking in the woods but has a hard time getting away for the summer. He recently told me how much he loves his work, how, even though the needs of the homeless are never-ending, he wakes up every morning increasingly motivated to do a little more to help. "Homelessness doesn't take vacations, so neither can I."

Dave was one of a great many students whose lives changed course after taking Professor Wiesel's class. Tracy put aside a career in finance and decided to study journalism. She focuses on reporting untold stories of marginalized communities — immigrants and refugees, mostly, as well as youth at risk. At one point in her career she traveled to Lebanon and Syria to find refugees trapped by war in order to share their stories with the Western world. She told me, "I still remember: I sat in his class, and I felt my future changing as he spoke."

Miriam is a priest who works with mentally ill homeless people, using poetry and fiction to empower them. When she feels her patience fraying or when she witnesses the disturbed and feels afraid, she hears Professor Wiesel in her mind saying, *Breathe . . . and listen.*

Another student, Mohamed, went back to his native Pakistan to work for human rights, especially those of women targeted by their own families for perceived sexual improprieties. A fourteen-year-old rape victim threatened by her parents with stoning; a woman blinded in an acid attack; a survivor of an honor-killing attempt — Mohamed tries to help them. He wrote to Professor Wiesel over many years with questions and seeking encouragement as he endangered his life helping women at risk. In one letter he wrote, *I am able to help a handful of women and girls. But I can do nothing to change the reality here. It is hard, and I am trying not to give up. Your words against despair are helping me.*

WHEN I ENCOUNTERED THESE students and their stories, the ways in which they were inspired to become activists of different sorts, I felt humbled, even ashamed. Wasn't I equally exposed to Professor Wiesel's message? Didn't I spend even more time with him over more years? Why, then, did my work remain in the realm of ideas? I was getting my PhD, becoming, as one of my children explained to a friend, "a doctor who doesn't help people." I began to look inside to try to understand what was getting in the way of my involvement in causes I cared about.

One day, I interrupted my regular meeting with Professor Wiesel to share my struggle. "I feel like a phony," I said. "I study and teach about humanism, yet I myself am not doing anything concrete to help. I don't travel to conflict zones. I don't write op-eds in newspapers. I don't open my home to refugees. And I am trying to understand why and what I can do to change this."

He looked at me and said, "First, you are being hard on yourself. You are more engaged in these issues than many people, and teaching *is* a form of activism. Do you think it doesn't make a difference? Each student you touch may work in more concrete ways than you, yet his or her work will be motivated by your encounters. Do not underestimate that."

AFTER DISCUSSING THE SITUATION in Darfur, Professor Wiesel tells a story. "A student once asked the famed rebbe of Kotzk, 'Why did it take God six days to create the world? Look at it—it's filled with corruption, cruelty, inhumanity!'

"The master replied, 'Can you do better?'

"The disciple said, 'I think—yes! Yes, I can!'

"The master said, 'So what are you waiting for? Get started! Go to work—immediately!'

"This is what I feel when I wake up. Another day, I've been given a life, I must do something with it. And there is so much to do."

Professor Wiesel nods at a grad student named Susannah, who says, "Professor, that's just it. There's so much to do. It's so overwhelming. How do we choose which issues to address, whom to help, *how* to help? Where do we start?"

"You start where you are," he says, turning his hand palm up. "What have you seen? Who are the human beings you pass on the street every day? My friend Abraham Joshua Heschel, the great theologian and civil rights activist, was for a time the head of the committee for prospective rabbinical students at the Jewish Theological Seminary in New York. Once, a student arrived for his interview, and Heschel asked him how he had traveled to the seminary. The student told him that he had walked a few miles, from the West 70s to 120th Street.

"Heschel said, 'Tell me, did you see the homeless woman on 96th Street? The one with the hand-printed sign and the blankets?' The student said he had not.

"Heschel said, 'Did you see the veteran on 117th? The man with a gray beard and few teeth; he usually wears a baseball cap?' Again, the student said he had not.

"'And the tall man with dreadlocks outside of Zabar's who stands with his hands in the air, praying?' Heschel asked. Once again, the student replied he had not noticed this man.

"Heschel said, 'How can you become a rabbi if you don't see the human beings around you?'

"You don't have to go far away, you just have to notice who is

around you, in your street, in your family, among your friends,"
Professor Wiesel continues. "What are their needs? What is
their pain? It can be small. Modest acts of kindness are more
significant than we recognize. It does not have to be newswor-
thy. You just need to look for the outstretched hand. You just
need to touch one person every day with compassion."

Walt, a retired academic dean who has attended Wiesel's
classes for over a decade, says, "My problem is, I do something
small, write a check or something, and I feel better. I don't
want to feel better; I want to hold on to the outrage so I can do
more. How do I do that?"

"The question is, how real are other people to you? Do you
feel their suffering? Does it actually keep you up at night? It
is not easy when we know how much suffering there is. We
can feel overwhelmed, as Susannah said. And you can remain
asleep to others' pain. We need to find a balance between sleep
and paralysis. Start with one person. A person is not an abstraction—we must be *against* abstraction. One million pairs
of shoes taken from children in the camps are a statistic; one
is a tragedy.

"But don't just write a check; help them somehow with
your own effort, your own energy. Buy them food and bring it
to them. Help them find shelter. Speak to them, take the time
to really speak and listen. Who will listen to them? We must be
the ones who do. This means that your feelings of anxiety or
calm, your presence or lack thereof for another person, your
smile at a fellow human being or your turning away, your feeling overwhelmed and how you manage that—all of these little, internal things contribute somehow to the destiny of the
world."

How Do We Know?

ONCE WE OVERCOME INDIFFERENCE, despair, and a sense of being overwhelmed by the world's problems, we still have challenges to face. One of them is epistemological, the challenge of clarifying the truth of a situation somewhere far away.

On a cold Boston morning, it is hard to imagine the intense heat of the refugee camps in Philip Gourevitch's *We Wish to Inform You That Tomorrow We Will Be Killed with Our Families,* his account of the Rwandan genocide. Gourevitch's book has made some students cry in class already, and others have said they have spent sleepless nights thinking about the murder of neighbor by neighbor. Now, in lecture, Professor Wiesel is drawing a parallel between two historical moments of moral failure.

"In *that* time, my own time, the government *knew,* it knew what was happening. Roosevelt knew. The Vatican knew. In London, Stockholm, Geneva, it was known. Only we Jews in Hungary did not know. When we arrived at Auschwitz, none of us recognized the name or knew what it meant. Why did the governments of the world not *do* something, at least to *tell* us?

"And here, again," he continues, "we have the same thing. We *knew* about Rwanda, yet the world did not intervene. The only difference, perhaps significant but certainly not sufficient, is that in this case, President Clinton at least acknowledged America's failure and apologized to the people of Rwanda. Most of the time, I feel my words have no real impact, but this time . . . our conversation inspired that apology. But it is not enough, cannot be enough."

Deborah, a journalism student, asks, "Professor Wiesel, what will it take for our country to step in the next time this happens somewhere? What will really make that difference?"

James raises his hand urgently. "Isn't it more complicated than that? I mean, yes, if we know there's a genocide happening, fine. But often we don't even know who the bad guys are or whether it's actually a genocide or a civil war." He is referring to the situation in Darfur, described by the government as a civil war and by human rights organizations as a genocide. I am suddenly more alert; this question has bothered me for years.

But Professor Wiesel replies, "We knew. We knew. It's true that sometimes we do not, but in the case of Rwanda, we had enough reports, enough clarity, to know."

James pushes back. "But what about when we *don't* know?"

Aimee, who has seemed agitated all morning, raises her hand. "Professor, in high school, I organized care packages for the refugee camps. My classmates and I sent seven hundred dollars' worth of supplies, blankets, canned goods, first-aid kits, to the camps. And in this week's reading I find out that our help went to the killers who were in charge of the camps. What are we supposed to do with that information? How can we ever know if we're actually helping or making things worse?"

We all can locate her question in this week's reading. Gourevitch wrote that, because malnutrition rates in the UN-run refugee camps were lower than in Rwanda itself, the camps attracted the guilty, the *genocidaires* who had killed their Tutsi neighbors. These fugitives often wound up running the camps. Some funds sent to the camps were used to buy weapons that were then funneled to Hutu rebels, who used them to ambush Rwandan convoys. Gourevitch wrote, "What made the camps almost unbearable to visit was the spectacle of hundreds of international humanitarians being openly exploited as caterers to what was probably the single largest society of fugitive criminals against humanity ever assembled."

Aimee is very disturbed by her tiny role in this, and the other students pick up on that. Many of them are looking at her, and I see them register the intensity of her feelings. Then all eyes turn back to Professor Wiesel.

He says, "You ask the question *because of* Gourevitch's book; therefore, you trust him as a witness, as a writer. Before you read the book, you did not know. Now that you know, you will act differently. But in both moments, your intention was to help."

He continues: "How do you know what to do? If you are not there to see for yourselves, how can you ever know what is happening on the other side of the world? You must first find those who have been there, witnesses who can describe what they have seen. But how do you know who is a true, an honest witness?"

He looks at James.

"Philosophers have asked similar questions before, about the nature of action and the nature of truth. How do you distinguish a true from a false prophet? The answer is, a false prophet comforts; a true prophet disturbs. You must ask: Is the witness telling you what you want to hear? Is he challenging you? And, of course, what does he stand to benefit from his own testimony?

"This question has its own life in metaphysics. Kierkegaard

famously asks how Abraham knew it was God telling him to sacrifice his son. He answers that it was the *same* voice as the one that called him to leave his homeland years earlier. But he warns that Moloch can imitate God's voice. Sartre asks how one is to know whether a voice that one hears at night is that of an angel or a pathology. After all, some of those afflicted with insanity also claim to hear God's voice!

"In fact, a Hasidic legend tells us that Satan agreed to God's plan to send great leaders down to this world only on one condition: that God would also send *other* leaders, individuals with the same charisma and charm, the same powers. God agrees and says to Satan, 'These leaders will have the same powers, the same charisma, as the others. Only I and you will know that they are really yours.'

"We have asked many times before, 'Where is Mephistopheles? Where is evil?' We know that evil is at its most dangerous when it hides itself and tries to appear as good. And we know that it is the killers who are often the most fanatical. They have convinced themselves of the justice of their cause, and so they will shout the righteousness of their cause. In fact, the only thing that can allow them to murder, especially to legislate state-sponsored murder, is a compelling and elegant idea. So cutting through to the truth is indeed difficult.

"Still, there are some things you can do. Read competing news sources, ones that disagree with each other vehemently. You will find some things they agree on, and these are more likely to be trustworthy elements. Convene people with very different perspectives and listen as they argue. Demand that they base their words on evidence, on facts, not just on opinion. Check the veracity of these facts. Question them and their agendas. Do not trust messengers who are too smooth, whose message is too perfect, too beautiful."

Then, still attuned to Aimee's sense of betrayal and disappointment, he turns to her. "Listen," he says. "I also have tried to make things better, to intercede, only to complicate matters. I will tell you of one of these moments. It is not an easy memory. You know, in 1992 I visited Yugoslavia with a small delegation. We went to bear witness, to see the victims of the war, to see the detainment camps, and to find out whether the reports of atrocities there were true. If they were, we would let the world know. We went to a camp called Manjaca, a place with a very bad reputation. There we met with prisoners. I demanded promises, oaths from the camp commander, Popovic, a man known as bureaucratic but reliable, that no one would be harmed as a consequence of speaking to us. And he gave his word. We spoke to fifteen prisoners, alone in an infirmary, without any guards present. Later we found out that those prisoners, the ones we interviewed, were transferred to a worse camp, with worse conditions, *because* they had spoken to us! I still feel responsible, to this day." (I later learned that he did get the Bosnian leader Karadzic to close the unheated Manjaca camp before the temperatures dropped dangerously and threatened the lives of thousands of Muslim prisoners.)

He pauses and gazes down at the dark wooden table for a long moment. He looks suddenly old. "And yet . . . what can we do? We can only do our best with what we have, what we know. We must ask, and ask, and ask again, and once we feel we have the knowledge we need, we must act. To avoid action for fear of causing more harm is to play into the hands of those who *deliberately* cause harm and who hope for our silence. We cannot do that."

Truth and Reconciliation

"DO YOU NEVER FEEL hatred for the German people?" asks Dietrich, a German graduate student focusing on Holocaust studies.

"You must turn hate into something creative, something positive. If you are a teacher, you turn it into good teaching. If you write, turn it into good writing. Express what you feel and let the hate become something else. But do not hate."

His hand drifts up to his cheek. "It's more than that, really. When I first met children of Nazi officers, young Germans who carried a burden of guilt and horror, I learned something. I had never before considered that it could be as painful to be the children of those who ran the camps as to be the child of those who died in them. But it is true. That is why many German students come to study here, or at Yad Vashem [the Holocaust education center in Jerusalem], or the Holocaust Memorial Museum in Washington. And they should be embraced. I do not believe in collective punishment. Each generation, each person, creates his or her own destiny. We are all, whatever our history and backgrounds, part of the same quest."

Emma, a theater major and aspiring actor, asks, "Is forgiveness possible?"

Professor Wiesel replies, "If someone harmed me, I might

forgive him. But who am I to forgive on behalf of the dead? Those who are not alive cannot choose to forgive, and I cannot decide that for them.

"Many years ago, several years after the war, I was living as a journalist in Israel. One day in Tel Aviv I was on a bus, and I saw a man. The first thing I recognized was his neck, because I was standing behind him. I knew that neck. It belonged to a Jewish guard from Auschwitz, a kind of collaborator.

"I approached the man and said, 'Were you in Germany during the war?' The man said yes. I asked, 'Were you in Auschwitz?' The man said yes. I asked, 'Were you at such and such a camp?' The man said yes. Then I asked, 'Were you at such and such a block?' And I described more and more specifically until the guard recognized me. And we both realized this man had been the guard at my barracks inside the camp."

Professor Wiesel looks up. "I knew in that moment that all I had to do was shout — Tel Aviv at that time was a place where this man would not be safe had the crowd known who and what he was, what he had done. I knew I could have had him arrested or worse, and all I had to do was to raise my voice. I held this man's life in my hands." His gaze returns to us. "I did nothing. I cannot call this an act of forgiveness. But it was an act of letting go. I am not a judge. I am only a witness."

A Leap of Hope

"AFTER ALL THAT HAS happened, genocide still is going on in the twenty-first century. If the world didn't change after Auschwitz, how could it ever possibly change? How can we have hope that it can change?" At least one student asks this question each semester.

Professor Wiesel replies now, "We must hope in spite of despair, because of our despair; we must not give despair the victory. I do not believe the world is learning. And I cannot hide from that fact. And yet, I do not believe in despair. People speak of a leap of faith. I believe we require a leap of hope."

"But do you see reasons for hope, evidence for it?" asks Abigail, a science major.

"What is the alternative? Camus said, 'Where there is no hope, we must create it.' We can always find hope. When the writer Tristan Bernard was arrested by the Gestapo, his wife noticed him smiling. She asked him why, and he said, 'Until now, I lived in fear; now I shall live in hope.' Even then, as he was being deported, he had a choice.

"History offers us hope as well. The Warsaw ghetto uprising was led by twenty-year-olds, and it took longer for the Germans to occupy the ghetto than it did for them to occupy France. The first recorded response of the Germans to that uprising was a Nazi officer who cried, 'Look, Hans, women are shooting!' In Auschwitz, a woman named Roza Robota smuggled grains of dynamite *under her fingernails* for weeks in order to collect enough to bomb the crematoria. She and others were responsible for the Sonderkommando Revolt in October of 1944. She and three other women were hanged, and as they were being executed, they shouted a biblical phrase: 'Be strong and of good courage!' There were many instances of resistance like this, and there is no resistance without hope.

"And I must tell you that even there, in the camps, I saw

kindness and goodness. I saw people encourage one another with words they could barely speak. I saw people pray in spite of God's absence. I saw a father give his son his last piece of bread, and I saw the son give it back. Prisoners tried to protect those who were weaker or too sick to work from the guards. That was a defeat of the enemy. The enemy tried to dehumanize us but succeeded only in dehumanizing himself. We, the victims, kept our humanity. Hannah Arendt" — the philosopher and author of *Eichmann in Jerusalem: A Report on the Banality of Evil* — "was wrong when she said we are all capable of evil. It is not true.

"In 1945, Jews came out of ghettos and forests. The partisans had guns; they could have set the world on fire. It didn't happen. With very few exceptions, they did not seek revenge. They sought victory through life. Survivors as a group have advocated hope, not despair; generosity, not bitterness; gratitude, not violence. They chose to have families, to rebuild decimated communities, to become philanthropists and doctors, to find a way to help others.

"There was a woman at Mount Sinai Hospital in New York, in the maternity ward. She was a survivor. The nurse who later told me this story saw her from the doorway, holding her newborn baby. And the woman held this baby up and said, 'See, world, I am not the last.' *That* is the revenge of the survivors — new life, new families, new communities, helping others, making the world better."

"Did you feel the same way about becoming a parent?" Abigail asks.

"For a time when I was younger, I thought I would never have children. How could I bring new life into a world that could allow such things to happen? But I changed my mind, thanks in part to the urging of my teachers, who pressed me over several years to reconsider. And I knew I must choose hope in spite of everything. I am very glad I did.

"And then there is today. Imagine the many factors that led to us being here together, to learn, to question, to meet one another. *You* give me hope, your sincerity, your quest for knowledge, for meaning. When two people come together to listen, to learn from each other, there is hope. This is where humanity begins, where peace begins, where dignity begins: in a small gesture of respect, in listening. Hope is a gift we give to one another."

He continues. "As we have seen, to turn away from reality, to pretend that evil is not evil, has one result: to empower evil. And yet, if we always look into the abyss, we will be tempted by despair. Hope is a choice, and it is a gift we give to one another. It can be absurd. It does not rely on facts. It is simply a choice. Once you make that choice, to create hope, then you can look at evil without flinching, without falling. And this is the first step to fighting it, to protesting it."

Dave says, "What should we tell the others, those outside this classroom?"

Professor Wiesel opens his hands in a pensive gesture. "Tell them we can do so much more. And since we can, we must."

6

Beyond Words

How can you sing? How can you not?

— ELIE WIESEL

ON A COLD DECEMBER morning in Boston, Professor Wiesel is singing to his students. He is singing a song from his childhood, conveying the beauty of a lost world. The song has no words—it is a *nigun,* a wordless melody—and it gives me chills. It shifts from a major to a minor key and back, and the effect is eerie and poignant. He is a lyric baritone with a strong yet delicate voice. His eyes are closed, and he sways with the rhythm of the melody. His hands move gently up and down, as if he is conducting an invisible choir. When the song picks up, he snaps his fingers, then claps his hands.

He ends the melody and waits a moment in silence before opening his eyes. He says, "This *nigun* of the Vizhnitzer Hasidim is the best way I know to return to my childhood. And to share it with you. Why do I tell you about Hasidism other than because it is an essential part of my childhood? Because Hasidism teaches how to build on ruins."

After class, I climb the stairs to his office and knock on his door.

"Professor, can I ask you a quick question?"

"Of course, just a moment," he says without looking up. He finishes writing something on a small piece of paper, then turns to me.

"I'm curious—why did you decide to sing today? You've never done that before, at least not while I've been your TA. It was beautiful, and moving, but . . . why today?"

He looks at me soberly and says, "Sometimes, we must move beyond words. As you know, teaching and learning do not happen only through the sharing of information; there must be an added element. I have been lecturing all semester, the students have been reading wonderful novels and plays, we have discussed and questioned. And yet I felt that something was missing: the melody. So I decided to sing."

I thought about this brief conversation over the next few weeks. Now that he mentioned it, I could see that this group of students had been less engaged than others in previous years. It was subtle, but it was so. That moment of song opened some hidden door, and in the class meetings that followed, the discussions were more alive; the students raised their hands more often, they asked deeper questions. It struck me that perhaps they began to share more of themselves because he had shared more of himself.

Language and Its Limits

PROFESSOR WIESEL CONSIDERED memory to be the essential ingredient in educating people toward humanity. His lifelong project was to transmit his experiences and their implications, to bear witness to the Holocaust, and, through that, to be a witness for others too. But he also acknowledged the limits of transmitting memories.

What do you do when you approach those limits? What do you do, as a writer and as a teacher, when words fail? This was not a theoretical question for him. He was torn between the need to share his Holocaust testimony with the world and the impossibility of doing so. How does one say the unsayable, convey the ineffable?

In a classroom lecture he says, "The original version of *Night*, which I wrote in Yiddish, was almost nine hundred pages long. And then, I cut, and removed, and pruned. Writing for me is not like painting; it is like sculpture. The sculptor sees an image within a piece of rock, and he carves away material to reveal that image. Flaubert once said, 'I spent the entire morning sitting before my novel, and added a comma. Then I spent the entire afternoon, and erased it.' That is how it is for me. I carve away words until what is left is the essential. But those other, erased, words are there."

"How are they there if you've erased them?" asks Alan, a lawyer and master's student from Washington, DC.

"They are present like the dead are present, though they are gone. But it doesn't happen by itself; it requires intention. I swore not to write of my experiences until ten years had passed."

Alan asks why.

"So that the silence too would be there, within each word."

"Why is that important?"

"Because words alone cannot convey the experience. The

killers found a language to describe what happened; the victims did not. I did not know — I still don't know — whether I could find the right words. Therefore, there must be silence if one is to have any hope of transmitting something that is beyond words.

"Look, language is essential. It is more than a vehicle to transmit ideas or memories; it is a desire of the human being to transcend his own limits. Language is composed of words but is more than words. It is also the white spaces between letters, words, people. When you read — or, better, see a performance of — *Waiting for Godot,* you notice that much of the action takes place between the scenes. The plot is so minimal, the characters sketched in such a spare way, that we cannot help but project our personalities, our wishes, onto them. It is a kind of personality test. The characters come in pairs, and there is always a space between them — pay attention to that space. That is where the mystery is.

"In literature, what we try to find is the secret place in the story — what is unsaid is more important than what is said. In history too. I am intrigued by Nikolai Gogol, the Russian playwright, for example. He went to Jerusalem, and when he came back, he burned the second volume of his play *Dead Souls* — why? And then there is Nietzsche, who became very ill in 1889, and from that moment on he did not write a single line. What happened to him in those eleven years before he died? What did he want to write and didn't? What went through his mind?

"The great stories are alive. They are moving, not fixed, not static. You can almost hear them breathing, and they enfold you. So that as you read, you find yourself inside Sophocles's imagination, inside Shakespeare's mind — and you are different, you have new thoughts and feelings. This is how moral evolution truly happens, not through natural selection but through stories.

"Therefore we must tell the stories. There is a Yiddish saying: 'God created the world because He loves stories.' Even God needed language to create the world. Since my childhood, I learned to respect language.

"But language can be corrupted. It can be contaminated by human cruelty. A Chinese legend tells us of a dragon that does not shed blood but nonetheless commits murder—with words. The language of the victimizer is not the same as the language of the victim. After the events of the twentieth century, words like *selection, collaborate, purify* take on new meaning. I cannot hear these words without shivering. Remember, when you read, that every sentence has a past. After the war, we were alienated from language. *Fire, hunger*—who can know what those words mean who did not experience what we have experienced? If I waited ten years before writing, it was because I wasn't sure I could find the words to communicate. Some writers like me committed suicide. Perhaps it is because they understood the frailty of language. And so sometimes you must reach beyond language, to silence.

"For myself as a writer, this is essential. Camus said, 'I entered writing through worship.' Others entered through anger. I enter through silence. There are many varieties of silence—that of consent, of confusion, of grief, of mystical experience. We have seen the silence between Cain and Abel, their inability to communicate, which led to history's first murder. There is the famous awkward silence, which many of us have experienced. And then there are some questions to which silence is the only answer, like Aaron's silence in the book of Leviticus when his two sons are killed when they bring a 'strange fire.' *VaYidom Aharon,* 'And Aaron was silent' — this was the only response to such a tragedy. But there are other forms of silence as well, which I have tried to explore in my books."

Isabel raises her hand. "You've talked here about *Night;* what about your other books? Is it the same when you write now?"

"Sometimes I worry that all my other books are jealous of my first. But, really, it is different, but there are connections. If not for my first book, I would never have written any others. But those books are celebrations, and questions. Each one is a different question: about power, about faith, about madness. If you have read any of my other books, you know that I don't write about it [the Holocaust] a lot. Why? Because I don't want it to become routine, banal. I want to tremble before I write the word *Auschwitz.* But it is there in all my books. I am the one who writes it. So it is there.

"The great danger is banality, that the words that should have the power to set the page on fire will become banal. That we will become desensitized. That is the reason I write, and teach — to avoid that. And because we rely on language, it is very possible for this to happen. I write what I write so that others will learn, so that things will be different. But, as you know by now, I am not convinced the world is learning anything. I have told you that Kafka speaks of the messenger who cannot deliver his message. But what of the messenger who *does* deliver his message, but nothing changes?

"There was an eighteenth-century Jewish jeweler named Oppenheim who once remarked: 'Who is a good businessman? To sell a jewel you own to someone who wants it does not take much skill. But to sell a jewel you *don't* own to some-one who *doesn't* want it—that's a good salesman!'

"The Hasidic master Rebbe Naftoli of Ropshitz was a great speaker, endowed with a superb sense of humor. One Shabbat before Passover, he came home from the synagogue. Customarily, the rabbi of the town must deliver a speech on that Shabbat about charity, about the need to help poor people who don't have enough money to celebrate the holiday, and he gave that speech. When he came home, his wife asked him, 'Nu, how was it?' He said it was okay. 'Well, did you accomplish anything?' He said, 'Only half.' She said, 'What do you mean?' He said, 'I did not succeed in convincing the rich to give, but I managed to convince the poor to receive.' I feel like that often. I am an outsider with some stories to tell. Some of them are beautiful; many are painful. I do not even speak or write in my mother tongue. Finding the words is the great challenge.

"It is even more difficult when we consider the weakness of language itself. For we have seen how the enemy manipulated language during the war."

"Do you mean propaganda?" asks Alan.

"That is a part of it, the identifiable aspect. The oppressor often obscures facts with contrived language. Beckett said, 'Language, like a prostitute, offers itself to whoever wants it.' It is very easy to distort. In war it is always language that dies first, is mutilated first, is violated first. In war, language becomes obscene, indecent, vulgar. How? It is simple. Orwell described this well, that words lose their meaning to their substitutes. Hitler referred to his anti-Semitic program as the Final Solution. Stalin used the term *popular democracy* to describe his satellites in Eastern Europe, even though they were neither popular nor democratic. Governments don't lie; they engage in *disinformation*. Revolution? Oh no, don't call it that, call it *destabilization*. Third-world countries aren't poor, they are *underprivileged*.

"Part of our task is to liberate language, to name things as they really are. Don't say *income inequality* when you can say *hungry child*. Don't say *racial tension* when you can describe rocks thrown at a family. This is true in political life, in literature, and in education as well. We cannot liberate reality if we distort language."

I understood that, for Professor Wiesel, words were necessary but not sufficient. The reason he chose to sing in class was a response to big questions: *Have we succeeded in transmitting the message? No? Well, then, perhaps a song will succeed where words alone could not.*

ON A TUESDAY MORNING during my first semester as a teaching assistant at BU, Professor Wiesel asks me if I want any of the books he has set aside to give away because his library is slowly taking over several rooms of his office suite. Some of these are books sent by strangers with enthusiastic, sometimes overheated notes (*This sci-fi book will answer all your questions about faith!*), some are obscure works of history, and some are copies of books he already owns.

One Sunday morning a few weeks later, I pick up one of those books, a collection of Yiddish folktales. I open it to a fantastic story of a young woman named Sarah who is taken by a raven to the tip of the church tower and will not come down. When she eventually does decide to return home, her parents and her brother refuse to welcome her or allow her in. Finally, her sister invites her in, feeds her, and puts her to bed. I can't stop thinking about the story. Why is it her sister alone who welcomes her? What does it take to welcome back people who have gone to forbidden places? And if Freud was right that every character in a dream is the dreamer, what does it take to welcome back parts of ourselves that have gone astray?

The following night I am at dinner with my family. Over mac and cheese, and while feeding our toddlers (the baby is asleep), my wife and I are deciding whether to buy a new air conditioner or get our car fixed. One of the kids starts crying because he has gotten cheese all over his hair, so I pick him up, carry him to the kitchen sink, and give him a quick rinse in warm water. I make it a game and he laughs. In the midst of all of this, an image forms in my mind: Sarah from the Yiddish story, hanging by her shirt from a weathervane on the church tower, watching as the raven flies away. I finish the impromptu bath and excuse myself, run upstairs to my small art studio, and hastily sketch this image. That sketch will become the seed for an illustrated book. It also opens the door to a lot of art-making.

Over the next few weeks, though I am usually exhausted at the end of the day from my studies and the demands of parenting small children, I spend hours late at night in my little studio drawing, experimenting with layouts, colors, and different media. I feel like I did when I was a child coming home from school to draw, losing track of time. *When did I last lose myself in art-making?* Suddenly I realize that it's been at least five years, because the entire time I was in yeshiva, I didn't create any art.

I hadn't registered this before. Art had once been such an es-

sential part of my life. I knew of returnees to the faith who renounced their previous lives and the creative expressions that
had once defined them: musicians who stopped playing music,
dancers who stopped dancing. But for me, choosing not to create was not a conscious decision; it just happened, without my
even noticing.

It took me almost a year to develop some clarity about this.
I eventually realized that the rigors of my education and an
ethos that privileged Talmudic study over all else had taken
their toll. I felt guilt for every minute I wasn't immersed in the
sacred texts. Add to that my commitment to my young family
and the demands of married life, especially one built around
traditional Jewish practices, and I could understand why art
took a back seat for me.

But I intuitively felt there was more to it, and I was able to
articulate that missing element only when I read an essay by
the Jungian psychologist Erich Neumann on the modern Jewish artist Marc Chagall. The Jewish people, wrote Neumann,
did not have a fully developed visual tradition because they
were a people formed in the desert. Their encounter with God
in the searing heat burned away all color. According to Neumann, it was not until Chagall that the Jews found color again.

Of course, this was an exaggeration, and there are many
beautiful decorative-art traditions from Jewish communities
around the world. But the idea struck a chord. This was what
happened with me, I realized; in my search for God and unadulterated, all-encompassing spirituality in a hilltop yeshiva,
my colors — my individuality, my passion for art, my natural
sense of freedom — were burned away. How could I draw or
paint without color?

Now, through the story of Sarah and the church tower, my imagination had been reactivated; my colors were starting to come back, and I was drawing again. I realized now why this story had such a hold on me: I unconsciously saw Sarah, the exiled, marginalized character, as a symbol of what I had exiled—my art. Sarah's sister welcoming her home represented my need to open the door to my art, my quirky individuality, to feed it and shelter it again. My notes from Professor Wiesel's classes during this period were filled with doodles and scrawls, faces in pencil and pen, shaded, fading into the background, morphing into other shapes and forms. I thought about my language-loving mother, my artist father, and my struggle to honor both of their gifts to me.

Now, steeped in language and literature in graduate school, I was ferociously thirsty for art and music, and over the next months, images exploded out of me, as if my freedom depended on coloring in every surface around me. At night, instead of putting my children to sleep with just a kiss and a hug, I started playing guitar and making up stories for them. They loved listening to the tale of Irv the Crocodile and the ongoing adventures of the Diaper Ducks. (Years later my youngest told me he thought those were characters and plots from an actual TV show.) I was welcoming Sarah back home.

IT IS A RAINY November morning in 2004, and I'm grateful for the heat in this large classroom. Still, Professor Wiesel is wearing a scarf, and he pauses often to clear his throat. He is continuing to discuss the gap between language and reality.

"A few words can tell of a million deaths," he begins. "Emanuel Ringelblum was one of the great chroniclers of Jewish life in the Warsaw ghetto—please read his book *Notes from the War-saw Ghetto*, it is important. And when you do read it, you notice something unbelievable: between two commas, ten thousand people burned. It costs so little to describe something whose cost cannot be measured. What does this tell us about language, about words, and about the role of the witness?"

Diana raises her hand. "It tells us that there's no possible way to really bear witness. Words fail, by their very nature. But you've spoken about the witness so much—how is anyone ever supposed to be able to bear witness?"

Rather than answer, Professor Wiesel looks expectantly at his class, waiting for them to respond. A student named Joshua does. "It's impossible to fully convey any experience, but if we didn't try, if we didn't at least approximate it, we'd have no literature, no religions, no movies or art . . . I think the point is to make the attempt, knowing it won't be perfect but doing our best with as much integrity as we can."

"Very good," says Professor Wiesel. "I need more."

I watch the students think.

Amber says, "Maybe writing is an act of protest, regardless of the results."

Nathan asks whether writing is meaningful without an audience. Professor Wiesel responds, "The authors of books buried during the Holocaust thought so. Though they had no idea if their words would be found, they wrote; they had to write. One of these, Chaim Kaplan, one of the great diarists of the Warsaw ghetto, asked, 'What will become of my diary?' That question is answered every time one of you reads it.

"We find the same thing with many other authors whose books were banned, censored, or burned. To understand a tyrant or tyrannical government, look at which books they ban, which books they don't want you to read." He turns to me. "In fact, Ariel, this would be a very good course for next year. Let's study banned and hidden literature." I make a note. (This is indeed one of the courses the following year.)

"I don't know," says Karen. "Sharing testimony seems essential, and it also seems futile. This feels like a Catch-22."

"It is!" says Professor Wiesel. "Words have tremendous power. Two hundred years ago, a revolution began with words. Diderot and Voltaire wrote a dictionary, and out of their words the French Revolution emerged. During the occupation, Albert Camus was in a café in France and heard a group of young students talking. They were fashionable, bohemian, and so of course they were existentialists. They were speaking of despair, the meaninglessness of life. Then several German officers came in, and Camus saw one of them point to a young man and tell him to follow. The officer took the young man outside and had him stand against the wall. He said, 'Repeat what you just said.' The young man stammered, 'L-life is meaningless.' The German aimed his gun at the student and said two words: 'Is it?' Camus said that he hated to learn something from a Nazi but that the lesson was important nonetheless.

"In spite of their limits, in spite of their vulnerability, words must be taken seriously. Camus retold this story because he knew this and wanted others to know. And yet, if the Holocaust proved anything, it is that the same person can love poems and kill children. We must always remember that a single life is worth more than all the words that have been written about life."

Is Art Incorruptible?

"CAN AESTHETICS GUIDE US where ethics has failed? Can beauty save us? Is song incorruptible?" In October of 2005, Professor Wiesel opens a lecture on the Russian poet Anna Akhmatova with these questions. "We need to show the inherent necessary connection between ethics and aesthetics. To show that doing right is beautiful, and that beauty leads us to the right. I am trying to teach you beauty. But it is not always simple. Ethics itself can be separated from what is right."

He arches an eyebrow and I know he's going to tell a joke. "At Hebrew University there was a professor who taught ethics. Suddenly, during a lecture, he turned to a student and said, 'Moshe, you are a poet, you have no money; my advice is that you marry a rich girl.' The student said, 'Professor, how could you say that, you, a man who teaches ethics?' The professor replied, 'Next door, Professor Frankel is teaching mathematics. Does he look like a triangle?'" The students laugh, and Professor Wiesel continues. "You see, any system of knowledge or behavior can be distorted if we are not careful to take it seriously and apply it with integrity. But what about art?"

He asks us to focus our attention on a poem Akhmatova wrote in 1916 entitled "Song About Songs," which ends with these lines:

> And so that I may lift
> My eyes in thanks to You above,
> Let me give the world a gift
> More incorruptible than love.

"Akhmatova suffered under the Communist regime. Her son was imprisoned in the infamous Lubyanka prison, and she did not learn his fate for months. In order to get her son released from prison, she was forced to write poems praising Stalin. She later requested that they not be published. But she never left Russia. Several of her friends, other famous poets, were arrested, some executed. In spite of, or perhaps because of, those experiences, in this poem she claims that song is 'more incorruptible than love.' Is this true?"

Marina, who was born in the former Soviet Union, is skeptical. "Hasn't beauty often been used to oppress? Aren't there entire industries dedicated to selling expensive and morally toxic products to naive people? Don't governments use spin to persuade people of the justness of their ideologies? Haven't tyrants built state committees of advertising, marketing?"

Professor Wiesel, perhaps picking up on her accent, asks her, "Have you experienced this directly?"

"No," she says, "because we moved here when I was only one year old. But my parents told me a lot of stories, mostly about how bad Russian art was. It was so ideological that whatever technical skill was used to make it was overshadowed by the moral ugliness, the lack of truth in it. They also told me a joke about the two Russian newspapers, *Pravda* and *Izvestia*, which mean 'Truth' and 'News.' The joke went, 'There is no *Pravda*, truth, in *Izvestia*, the news; and there is no news, *Izvestia*, in *Pravda*, the truth.'"

"That is a well-known joke, and it was true, and not only of newspapers," replies Professor Wiesel. "Look at Soviet-era artworks; they are some of the most depressing visual artifacts ever created. To use art to further a fascist agenda is a betrayal of beauty, and this inevitably affects the art produced under such regimes.

"Sometimes it is worse; sometimes the art itself is used to make killing easier. At Auschwitz, at the train depot, classical music was piped through the speakers in order to keep victims calm until they were through the gates and separated for processing, for selection! The music was the same as when it was written. But it was used as a tool to make murder easier."

Dan, whose grandmother is a Holocaust survivor, says, "Didn't the Nazis also have Jewish prisoners perform for visiting dignitaries to fool them into thinking the camps were not so bad? And didn't at least one SS officer listen to music while practicing his shooting skills on Jewish inmates?"

Amy adds, "In Rwanda, Philip Gourevitch reports that the most popular song on the radio in 1993 or 1994 was called 'I hate Hutus.'"

The evidence mounts. The case against the incorruptibility of art is strong. But Jason, whose grandfather is a survivor, also speaks up: "But isn't it also true that prisoners created their own music in secret? Wasn't there an entire culture of Jewish art, music, and theater right under the Nazis' noses? Wasn't their art a form of resistance?"

Professor Wiesel says, "You are right. In Buchenwald, children wrote poetry. In Theresienstadt, they became painters. In Lodz, there was a theater. There were high schools in the ghettos, weddings, children . . . they went on studying and singing. Their art was resistance. In general, art has its own inherent power and the intention of its creator. Nevertheless, it can be tainted by misuse, which is why knowing the history of works of art is important. For example, I would not go to a concert of Wagner's music. I have friends who do not agree with me, but personally I cannot do it. He was such a vicious anti-Semite. I have debated this with Daniel Barenboim, the conductor, who wanted to perform a concert of Wagner in Israel. There were survivors in the orchestra! This is a personal example; you must make your own choices. But you must know what the music, or art, or play was intended to convey and whether it was used in the service of humanity or its opposite before you decide."

Sing a New Song

IN SPITE OF HIS wrestling with the relationship between ethics and aesthetics, Professor Wiesel had a profound love of music. I discovered this on an early Tuesday morning in December 2005, two years into my tenure as his TA. After our usual discussion of the syllabus and course readings, he asked me, "What are you doing over vacation?"

I told him that, among other things, I was attending a choral concert, where one of my father's pieces would be performed. "Yes, I remember, your father is a composer. What is the composition?"

I told him the name of the piece, then shyly sang a few bars. Professor Wiesel listened, then came around his desk and gave me a hug. He had never done this in all these years; he had always greeted me with a handshake. "Thank you," he said.

Then he told me, "You know, as a child, I learned the vio-

lin, though I was never very good at it. And the melodies, I remember the songs we sang around the Shabbat table. I always,
always have a melody in my mind. It usually stays with me for
a few days, sometimes longer, until another comes to take its
place."

"What song do you have on the inner radio now?" I asked,
smiling, and he told me: "Eleh Chamdah Libi" ("These My
Heart Desires"), a celebratory tune sung on the autumn holiday of Simchat Torah, which also happened to be his Hebrew
birthday.

In a later classroom lecture, Professor Wiesel said, "After the
war I became a choral conductor, and I had a sixteen-person
choir. And the girls were very beautiful; they were so beautiful that I fell in love with them consecutively, one after the
other. The problem was, I was so timid I never told anyone.
At that time I needed, not to *be* loved, but to *love*. Therefore,
I celebrate love to this day." (He did indeed; he was thrilled
when couples met in his classroom. In one case, Professor
Wiesel coached a shy young student to leave a single rose on
his crush's chair on the last day of class. This couple later married, and they had two children who knew that Elie Wiesel
was their parents' matchmaker. Another time, Professor Wiesel entered his office in the early morning, out of breath from
climbing the stairs. He stared at his assistant for a moment, and
then asked about his date the previous evening. "This girl . . .
last night! Do you . . . like her?" The young man replied that
he could imagine being very happy with this woman. "Good!
That's . . . very good, really . . . good!" And he walked out, still
breathing hard, with a big grin on his face.)

Professor Wiesel continued. "In my tradition, music is very important. The Torah, the tradition itself, is called a song in Deuteronomy. Certain legends say that God created the world with song. The Psalms, of course, are central to Judaism, and to Christianity as well. In addition to its poetry, it calls upon the believer to 'sing a new song' to God, because to be creative is a religious demand.

"And then, in Jewish legend, song plays a role again and again. Moses was a stutterer until he sang at the Red Sea, when he became suddenly eloquent. And it is true that stutterers often don't stutter when they sing. It is said that King Solomon, wisest of men, knew the songs of the birds and could interpret them. Much later, a Hasidic master and his student were walking in the forest, discussing this legend. The disciple asked how one could learn the language of the birds. The master replied, 'When you know what your own soul is singing, you will also understand the songs of the birds.' We find similar stories about Saint Francis, and in Sufism, which teaches that Muhammad understood the birds as well.

"Song is so important that, according to one legend, the destiny of the world depended on it. In the second book of Kings, when Hezekiah, king of Judah, was saved from a foreign army, the rabbis comment that he was meant to be the Messiah, but because he did not sing in response to being saved, he did not fulfill his destiny, and the world remained unredeemed. Music is not an optional activity!

"Rebbe Pinchas of Koretz said, 'Ah, if only I could sing—I would force the Almighty to join us here on earth. But alas, I don't know how to sing.' And the first rebbe of Lubavitch said,

'When I cannot answer a question, I sing a song.' Music is a
miracle. For my generation, it is a miracle that we can sing."

For Professor Wiesel's seventieth birthday, several of his students surprised him in his office with a sing-along party. When
he saw them gathered there, he began leading a call-and-re-
sponse song, "Tzaveh Yeshuos Yaakov" ("Command Salvation for Jacob"), then another, "Shebishiflainu" ("In Our Low-
liness God Remembered Us"), and yet another, songs from his
youth, traditional melodies of the Vizhnitzer Hasidic group
into which he was born, and songs he learned later in Israel.
The singing went on for over an hour.

In class a student named Margaret asked him whether he
loved music for its own sake or for its ability to express what
couldn't be expressed in words.

He said, "Both, of course, and more. After the war it gave
me hope. It contains yearning for the past, and even if the past
is gone, lost, it still exists in the song. After all, the music of
exile is different from the music of home. And yet it can contain joy in spite of everything. You know, after the destruction
of the Temple in 70 of the Common Era, many of the leading rabbis decreed that Jews would no longer make music. For
many years, this was the rule in exiled Jewish communities.
Maimonides and others record this ruling in their legal works.
But how could we survive without music? Therefore, first only
at weddings, later as a general rule, music was allowed again.
After certain experiences, how can you sing? How can you
not?"

Mother Courage: Pleasure and Revulsion

"HOPE AND DESPAIR ARE two sides of a coin. We need hope to encounter despair—and keep going."

We are again discussing *Mother Courage and Her Children*, the play by the early-twentieth-century playwright Bertolt Brecht. The play takes place during the Thirty Years' War and is notable for the lack of even a single sympathetic character. After the play's opening, Brecht complained that the audience was too sympathetic to the character of Mother Courage.

"Brecht was an exile from his native Germany; he fled with the rise of the Nazis. He was troubled by the feeling that he had abandoned his fellow citizens, and he sought a way to communicate his solidarity with them across the great distance—through words," Professor Wiesel explains.

Ben, an outspoken sophomore, raises his hand. "Professor, I don't really understand the purpose of this play. It kind of winds down. It's depressing, with loss after loss, death after death. What's the message?"

Professor Wiesel nods. "Is it a tragedy or an antiwar statement? What is the purpose of a play about war? It is to force us to ask questions about the purpose of war itself. Brechtian theater, unlike Aristotle's theory of theater as catharsis, exists to *disturb*, to force the viewer to choose a side. We are meant to exit the play filled with a kind of internal pressure, which forces us to act against tyranny. We are not meant to feel better for having seen this play. We are meant to act."

Kayla and Peter raise their hands, and Professor Wiesel nods to Kayla. To Peter he says, "You are next."

"I was disturbed because I found the play beautiful," Kayla says, "even though it's an examination of war and it's very violent."

Peter agrees. "This is what I wanted to say too. Several of our readings have that quality of being readable, enjoyable as literature, while portraying disturbing events. I'm not complaining. I'd rather read a good book than a boring one, but when that happens I'm not sure how I should feel about enjoying the work."

I can tell that Professor Wiesel is pleased by this question.

"It is a work of art," he begins, "and art has its own logic; it has rules, and it breaks rules. It has rules: Chekhov said, if there is a pistol hanging on the wall in the first act, it must be fired in the third. And it *breaks* rules too, the usual ways we communicate: it can be beautiful when discussing ugliness, engaging when it portrays evil. We may even find ourselves enjoying characters' suffering. It may make us accomplices if we are not careful. You are implicated as you read. Some authors do this intentionally, to make you aware of your responsibility in life as in art. Art offers a distorted mirror to reality, and if you are responsible when reading fiction or a play, you are certainly responsible in actual life. Brecht is one of these authors.

"In great art, you may feel that your life is expressed better by the artist than by you. Goethe said that life is a fragment of something much larger that can be expressed only through art. I cannot accept this. Life is the end, not a means to an end. In a few words, a novel or play can tell us of hundreds or millions of deaths. But a single death is an unimaginable tragedy."

"How do you choose whether to write a novel or a play?" Marc asks. He is a playwright with a minor in philosophy.

"Sometimes a novel will simply be too long to explore a theme, and it must be a play. A novel can distract; one can become besotted with the form itself and lose the message. This is like the story of a man who was so in love with a certain woman that he sent her letters every day. And she fell in love . . . with the mailman! Theater can strip away excess, can reduce a tale to its essentials so the words do not distract from the message—they communicate it.

"But beyond this, theater is different because it creates a life, or an entire world, for an evening. Theater is a lie for the sake of truth, a truth that cannot be expressed in any other way. In theater, great theater, the characters speak *to* us because they speak *for* us. And its form mirrors its message. In *Mother Courage,* for example, Katarina is mute, because words fail. And Brecht uses not a flute, but a drum. Not music—war. The author is telling us that we must know when to play the flute and when to play the drum. The world has failed many times, playing music instead of working to prevent death. Brecht uses a language other than words.

"By the way, I must tell you that I love theater, and I love music. But I do not love them together. I find the music takes away attention from the power of the words, and the plot makes it difficult to appreciate the music. But in *Mother Courage,* the characters are singing only in order to push you away! You are not supposed to enjoy it; you are meant to be repulsed. Nietzsche said certain literature can either kill you or resurrect you. For Brecht, art must correct injustice. So it depends what you do with it. If you treat it as entertainment, it will destroy; if you allow it to change you, so that you begin to change the world around you, it can bring you to new life."

"Campo dei Fiori": Light a Better Fire

A FEW WEEKS AFTER the lecture on Akhmatova, we are discussing the Polish poet Czeslaw Milosz's poem "Campo dei Fiori," which deals with the martyrdom of Giordano Bruno in 1600 and connects it to the Warsaw ghetto, which Milosz, who aided Jews during the Holocaust, knew well. Bruno, a philosopher, theologian, and astronomer whose theories were anathema to the Catholic Church of his time, was found guilty of heresy by the Inquisition for his radical theology (he also supported the Copernican view of the solar system and claimed that stars were other suns with other, probably inhabited, worlds, and he believed in reincarnation). His trial lasted for seven years. Professor Wiesel asks a student to read Milosz's poem (the version below was translated by David Brooks and Louis Iribarne).

> In Rome on the Campo dei Fiori
> baskets of olives and lemons,
> cobbles spattered with wine
> and the wreckage of flowers.

> On this same square
> they burned Giordano Bruno.
> Henchmen kindled the pyre
> close-pressed by the mob.
> Before the flames had died
> the taverns were full again,
> baskets of olives and lemons
> again on the vendors' shoulders.

I thought of the Campo dei Fiori
in Warsaw by the sky-carousel
one clear spring evening
to the strains of a carnival tune.
The bright melody drowned
the salvos from the ghetto wall,
and couples were flying
high in the cloudless sky.

Those dying here, the lonely
forgotten by the world,
our tongue becomes for them
the language of an ancient planet.
Until, when all is legend
and many years have passed,
on a new Campo dei Fiori
rage will kindle at a poet's word.

Professor Wiesel thanks the student reader and says, "Milosz depicts the great distance between suffering and those oblivious to suffering. 'Before the flames had died / the taverns were full again' — how can it be that you witness an execution and go back to your drinking? How can it be that, a few blocks away, people are starving, and you are at a carnival? Milosz may have known that one year before he wrote this poem, a Vatican leader, Cardinal Mercati, discovered new documents related to the trial of Bruno and insisted that the Catholic Church was justified in burning him at the stake.

"'The bright melody drowned / the salvos from the ghetto wall' — Milosz knows that melody is a delicate thing and that a poem is not usually enough to save lives. But as much as he is aware of this weakness, Milosz knows the power of language. He imagines—fearfully—a 'new Campo dei Fiori,' but this time the poet will not be impotent to stop the flames. Instead, 'rage will kindle at a poet's word,' and his fire will overwhelm the fire of the auto-da-fé. As if the universe is defined by a war between two types of flame. One flame is intolerance, inquisition, the fire that is lit beneath the feet of innocent victims. What is the other flame?"

As the students digest this question, Professor Wiesel waits patiently, his hand resting on his cheek. Seconds pass, and Sean, an athlete who always wears flip-flops and sunglasses and has never spoken in class before, surprises me. "Isn't it passion? Feeling so strongly about something that you're on fire for it?"

"Exactly—you get an A plus, right away," says Professor Wiesel, smiling. Sean blushes. "So often we are told not to be too passionate, not to feel too much, to go along with the world as it is. I reject that. I believe we are meant to feel strongly, to feel deeply, to awaken and cultivate our yearning for good. Only then can we have a chance of overcoming those who are passionate for the wrong things.

"There is a story about the great author Isaac Babel. He was a lieutenant in the Russian cavalry. That cavalry conquered many areas of White Russia, Ukraine, and even Poland. Babel was a bloodthirsty fighter, an expert horseman and sharpshooter. One day he came to Chernobyl, a small town in Poland, and he heard that the last Chernobyler Rebbe was there. And even though he was in the Russian army, he had not forgotten his Jewish roots. He decided he would go to the old master and tell him that Jewish history was over, that religion was over, that now was the dawn of a new human age.

"He came to the master's house, and it was empty. Everyone was hiding in caves from the Russian army. He looked in room after room: no one. Eventually, he reached the study, and the rebbe was there, studying Talmud. He was so engrossed in his book that he did not notice the soldier staring at him. Babel was awestruck by the concentration he saw, and he just stood there for long minutes, staring. Finally, the rebbe noticed him. He assumed that anyone who came to him came as a supplicant, and in spite of Babel's uniform, he saw that he was a Jew, so he said, 'My dear Jew, what can I do for you?'

"Babel forgot what he'd been planning to say. He forgot that he was a lieutenant in the Russian army. He wrote, 'Suddenly a cry that was not mine came out of my mouth, perhaps it was my grandfather's. I heard myself say, "Rebbe, please give me fervor!"'

"Really, how can we live without fervor? And we have lost it; we do not even seek it as a society anymore. We have entertainment instead, distraction. Believe me, the Nazis, the Communists, the Khmer Rouge were passionate. They had a vision and were able to exercise power over their own peoples' profound longings — for ethnic purity, for an end to class warfare, for a new beginning to history, for religious hegemony. They had fire. It is not enough to be lukewarm in fighting such things; you must light a better fire."

The Return of Color

ONE MORNING IN OCTOBER I go to Professor Wiesel's office for our regular meeting. In the outer office, Detective Ryan of the Boston Police Department nods hello. Professor Wiesel has a security detail wherever he goes ever since several threats and a kidnapping attempt by a young Holocaust denier in San Francisco nearly a year earlier.

He welcomes me with a smile and shows me to my usual seat. He sits across from me and asks how I am feeling. I tell him that my grandfather is in the hospital, and I ask him to keep him in his thoughts and prayers. *"Refuah shlemah,"* Professor Wiesel says, the traditional Hebrew phrase that means "a complete healing."

I tell him that an exhibit of my artwork will be opening next week in Cambridge, the first exhibit I have had since age seventeen. Since I began making art again over a year ago, I have been prolific, and some of my work has attracted attention. To my surprise, Professor Wiesel says, "Good, I will come see your show." We set a date and time after work on the following Monday, then turn to the main subject of this meeting, a directed study he has agreed to do with me on the topic of social ethics.

When that Monday arrives, I meet Professor Wiesel outside his office. We leave the building and get in the private car he uses to travel in Boston. Detective Ryan is driving, and we make small talk for a few minutes. I thank him for doing this, and he says, "Of course. I'm happy to see your artwork." He adds playfully, "Maybe you will give me a gift of one of your paintings." I tell him it would be an honor. We arrive at the exhibit space, which is empty at the moment except for an administrator working at a desk in a back office.

Professor Wiesel spends a few minutes looking at each of the twenty or so pieces, a series of faces painted with different degrees of abstraction. I see him stand for a long time in front of one small piece, an abstract representation of a face done in black and white. It's minimalist and painterly, and though I'm right-handed, I painted it with my left, an attempt to let go of intentionality and control.

After another ten minutes or so he walks over to where I'm waiting and says, "That one is my favorite." "Why?" I ask, pleased. "It's *art*," he says enigmatically. I have no idea what he means, but I just thank him again for coming and walk him back out to his car, then I catch the train home.

Later, it occurs to me that this most spare of my paintings mirrored his approach to writing: the stripping away of anything inessential. Much of my work in this exhibit was layered, had accrued detail and texture through the application of paint, graphite pencil, and oil pastels. But the one he stayed with longest was simple, spare; it didn't have a single extra stroke. Of course he would like that one best.

His interest in my work crystallizes something for me. After years of absorbing words and ideas in yeshiva and then graduate school, I now feel able to express myself through word *and* image. And the fields of color, the textures, and the lines give the words deeper meaning.

For the Love of Chocolate

A FEW WEEKS LATER, in Professor Wiesel's outer office, I see
the two middle-aged women, teachers from Maine, who visit
every year and bring him fudge. When I see them waiting with
that box, I smile. They know the secret to Professor Wiesel's
heart: he loves chocolate. He has to be reminded to eat actual
food. In all my years as his TA, I only once saw him eating a
sandwich. I often saw him eat chocolate or chocolate rugelach.

When the women leave, twenty minutes later, I poke my
head into his office and ask if he is ready to see me. He is, and I
sit down with him at the small table by the bay windows.

"Ariel—what is happening with you?" he asks.

I tell him that I've begun teaching classes to adults in the
Jewish community as a way of putting myself through school,
and this has raised questions. "How do I know when I am really ready to teach?" I ask.

"You teach when you cannot *not* teach," he replies. "When
you feel that you are overflowing, that if you give, it will not
take anything away from you, that is when you must teach."

Professor Wiesel's assistant knocks on the door and tells
him there's a phone call. It is, of all people, the French prime
minister.

I say, "Shall I step out and give you some privacy?"

He says, "You know I have no secrets from you," and he
takes the call.

This type of exchange will be repeated many times over the
years.

When he is done, we resume. I ask my next question, the

harder one. "I do feel pulled to teach, and it's possible that I can increase my teaching work. But if I do so, I'd have to pause or drop out of the PhD program."

"Are you unsatisfied with your studies?" he asks me gently.

"No, I'm really not. I just feel responsible. I've been studying for so long, seven years in yeshiva, three years here, I feel I need to be giving more."

"I don't think the PhD will be wasted," he replies. "You will give plenty. I will support you whatever you decide, but if I were you I might consider waiting a year or two. Soon you will complete your course work and take your comprehensive exams. Once that's done, you will have a lot of flexibility as you write your dissertation. During that time, you can also teach more in the community. What I see is good. You know where you're going, and to have both ordination and a degree will help you get there."

This resonates with me, and I say so. I also tell him that I feel I'm getting older, and the desire to build something feels increasingly urgent. The responsibility to share what I've learned is almost overwhelming.

"You will, Ariel. You're thirty-one?"

"I just turned thirty-two," I say.

"You are still young, although I know it doesn't feel like that. I have always felt old, that time is short, life is urgent. You are the same. But you have time, and you will find a way to share your voice. Your voice is as important as mine."

Art and Suffering

"MY TEACHER SAUL LIEBERMAN said, 'Someone who is not torn is not human.' Must art emerge from suffering?"

It's a bright day in Boston, and a ray of sunlight reflected from a window across the street is blinding some of the students. Though it's the middle of lecture, I get up and close the venetian blinds behind the professor.

A grad student named Jordan says, "I think it's a myth, the myth of the suffering artist. We don't think of the suffering doctor or lawyer—why should an artist be any different? Each person has work to do in his or her field. It's about discipline, learning a skill or craft. You can be happy and do that."

Susan, an art student, says, "But there is something about what your teacher said. When you're broken open by something, whether it's painful or joyous, something deeper can get out. It goes back to feeling deeply. I don't want to believe that it's suffering that makes great art, but there's something in it . . ."

Professor Wiesel says, "My own belief is that it is not necessary, and we should not seek it—there is enough without it—but suffering does serve an important function. It imbues one with authenticity, reveals it, actually, strips away the masks we use to hide ourselves from one another. It is difficult not to be naked when you are in pain. You might try to hide it, but those who know you well can see."

When he says this, I feel a sharp pang of recognition. I have spent much of my life working to present a facade of contentment when I have been anything but content. My art was in part a way of reconciling my parents' competing narratives, a way of transforming confusion into beauty. The core tension between two homes, text and art, tradition and creativity, has been the engine of all my searching, all my studies, all my creation. On another level, drawing and painting was a curious choice for someone with a blind sister—I made images she could never see. I realize that in a way, I have made art *for* my sister, creating the images she cannot. All of this runs through my mind as Professor Wiesel continues.

"We might ask, what else helps to strip away posturing, and what increases it?"

A student replies, "Well, I remember at the beginning of the semester you were talking about silence, in your writing and in general. I think being quiet, having time to do that, helps us to connect to our real selves and to not get distracted by everything that's going on around us."

"Good," says Professor Wiesel. "I need more."

"I think celebrity culture is a major issue," says Marina. "Some people make internet videos to try to become famous, and their life becomes a pose, imitating other celebrities. I think they lose their voice when they do this."

"I don't really know anything about the internet," says Professor Wiesel. "I barely know how to use a computer. But I understand your larger point. I will tell you a funny thing that happened to me. I was walking, and I passed a young couple. The girl said something to her boyfriend. I didn't hear, but from his answer I understood that she had said, 'I think that is Elie Wiesel.' *He* said, 'No, it can't be.' She came back to look at me, and then I heard her go back to him and say, 'You're right, it's not him!'" He chuckles quietly. "Really, I am glad. What would

I have done if they had recognized me? Do I need to sign an autograph to feel good? But I think those who are famous in spite of themselves can find ways to remain grounded. Silence does help, but there is one thing you didn't mention."

The class is curious, as am I.

"Friendship. Your friends keep you honest, if they are good friends; they help you stay close to your own voice, your truth. And the best music is polyphonic. There is a Hasidic teaching of Rebbe Nachman. He said, 'When two people speak simultaneously, there is dissonance. But when they sing together, there is harmony.' When the world loses its ethical compass, it needs beauty to recalibrate. When words fail, what is left to us but to sing?"

In Concert

IN 2010, HE PERFORMED an entire concert of songs from his childhood at the 92nd Street Y in New York. I sat in the third row with my daughter. He began by saying, "I hope you don't expect some kind of late-life career change; this is only once." And he sang, one song after another, mostly from his youth but a few from after the war, from the period when he was in the orphanage in France, with a choir accompanying him (conducted by my stepfather, Mati Lazar): "Rozhinkes mit Mandlen" ("My first lullaby," Wiesel said); "Oyfn Pripetshik" ("This is the first song I heard in *cheder*"), and many more.

"When we sang," he said, "the poor did not feel their poverty, and the sick didn't feel their sickness." He sang a song called "Es Brent"; its chorus was "Don't just stand there, brothers / Put out the fire, because our town is burning." Professor Wiesel said, "Each time I hear this song, it breaks my heart, and I think of the world, today, in danger. And what are we doing about it?"

After an hour and a half, he told this story: "In 1943 my mother took me to spend Shabbat with the Vizhnitzer Rebbe, and the rebbe's nephew was there. He had recently escaped from Poland, from Galicia, and everyone there begged him to tell of what he saw. The rebbe's nephew replied, not in words, but by singing this song."

And he sang "Ani Maamin" — "I Believe" — a song of faith in the coming of the Messiah. It contains the words "Although he will be late in coming, still I wait for him, expecting him every day."

He lingered a bit when he was done. Then he walked off the stage.

7

Witness

I learn and learn and learn, and I still feel like
I haven't even begun. But I will soon.

— ELIE WIESEL

IT IS THE LAST day of my final semester before graduating, and I am sitting in Professor Wiesel's office. We sit in our usual places at his small round table, with the sound of the cars outside providing a quiet counterpoint to our conversation. He turns to me and asks, "What course topics should I teach next year?"

I am surprised, because I won't be here.

I make a few suggestions, ideas for courses that were on my mind in past years but that for various reasons we never chose. The Biblical Imagination, Varieties of Mystical Thought, Faith and Destruction in Ancient and Modern Literature. He chooses this last for one of the courses, then adds, "What if I also teach a course on my own books?"

"You haven't done that in many years. Why now?"

He looks away and says, "I simply feel that it is time."

We are both still, allowing his statement to settle in.

"So," he says. "Ariel. We've done something good together."

I look at him and feel overwhelmed. I think of his first invitation to me when I was an undergraduate, my reluctant refusal, and my return to him. I say, "Thank you for waiting for me."

He understands. "I told you I would," he says, and he smiles.

We sit in silence for a few moments. Then Professor Wiesel asks me which job I've decided to take. For the past few months I've been weighing various options. One is a teaching position in a rabbinical seminary in New York, the second involves creating curricula for a national organization, and the third is a senior planning position in the local Jewish community. I tell him I am taking the third job.

"New York was just too expensive, and we can't afford to live there on a teacher's salary. The curriculum position is tempting, but I'm taking the planning job for two reasons. First, it pays better than the others, and I can't afford to ignore that now, with a growing family. And second, I think it will challenge me more than the others; it will give me a chance to make a difference beyond the classroom."

"It's good to be challenged, as long as you have *sipuk nefesh*," he says, using the Hebrew phrase meaning "deep personal fulfillment." He looks me in the eye for a moment, then continues. "But you are a teacher. So you should teach, even while you are working. Find a way to teach something, even one class, perhaps at your work, perhaps elsewhere."

It has not occurred to me to do this, but it sounds exactly right.

"You should really charge me for this advice," I tell him.

"But I know you couldn't pay me!" he says, laughing. Then he becomes serious. "I will help you whenever I can, you know that. For as long as God gives me years."

• • •

AS I LEAVE HIS OFFICE, I think about endings. Now that I'm getting ready to graduate, I wonder: How will I pass along what I've learned from Professor Wiesel, not only in his class but in our many conversations? I have now, after all, been his student for almost twenty years. What is my mission, as a witness to a witness?

Out of the Classroom

OVER THE FOLLOWING MONTHS, I travel to defend my dissertation in Professor Wiesel's New York office; graduate; and begin my new job.

The job involves a combination of community organizing, educational design, and marketing, and after years of study and being on the receiving end of the support that made my studies possible, I am thrilled to be giving back. I'm also grateful to be learning so much: about management, about organizational politics, about fundraising, and about design. All of this is a nice complement to my previous, much more metaphysical education, and I enjoy reading business-school articles and listening to interviews with successful entrepreneurs and incorporating what I learn into my work.

But I am also surprised to discover how much I miss teaching. Several times in the first weeks, when I wake up in the morning, it takes me a few moments to remember that I'm not going to the university today. Even though I've committed to teaching my first course at a local synagogue, I haven't started it yet, and I wonder if teaching one class on the side is going to be enough.

The potency of my desire to teach isn't the only surprise. When I receive my first paycheck in the mail, it's a shock—I didn't realize just how much would be taken out for health insurance, other benefits, and taxes. This becomes a source of tension at home as we register what this new life really looks like. I am gone much of the time, consumed by the complex and politically charged nature of my work, and we still aren't making ends meet. My wife supported my decision to take this job in part because we both thought it would help us save money and propel us into a solid financial situation for the first time. Now it looks like that is not going to happen. I start to wonder about the relationship between personal mission and taking care of family; it's hard to save the world when you have mouths to feed.

I'm so overwhelmed with work and these new struggles that I don't reach out to Professor Wiesel until a few months have passed.

I meet him in his New York office. There is no agenda, no course to prepare, no book list to finalize, no students whose needs we must attend to. I am here because I've missed him. And he seems different—he speaks to me as to a friend, though I can't think of myself as anything but his student.

He tells me of his work to build a coalition of government leaders willing to call out Iranian president Ahmadinejad for his Holocaust denial and his repeated calls for Israel's destruction. "We have learned to listen when someone uses such language. But it is always difficult to mobilize meaningful responses." He sighs and says, "We know so little. The older I get, the more I realize how little we know about ourselves, why we do the things we do."

"What do you mean?" I ask.

"We know so much about how hatred works," he says. "We know it starts with words, with symbols, and it ends with killing. We know this, we have seen it over and over, but we sit and watch as it happens yet again. Why? Because we are busy with our lives, because politicians want to win elections . . . I used to have more patience for all that."

He laughs at himself for getting wound up and then changes the subject. "Tell me what is new with you," he says, and so I tell him, with more candor than ever before, that we are struggling financially and that these struggles are affecting our peace of mind. I was taught that pursuing money was a distraction, yet I am finding that the real distraction is struggling to pay the rent.

"Money was a difficulty for me for many years," he says. "I wrote about it in my memoir. It's a part of life; you should not try to avoid it. But make sure you are spending at least some time advancing your vision for your life. Make sure you are developing, growing, and teaching. The financial stability will come. And, of course, let me know if I can help in any way."

His next question surprises me. "Who is your *mashgiach*?" (A *mashgiach*, a term used in traditional Jewish schools, is a kind of spiritual supervisor, a guide with whom students discuss personal issues.)

I think for a moment. "Well, *you* are."

Professor Wiesel says, "Now you need to develop your own, inner *mashgiach*."

I sit in his office feeling slightly deflated: Is he abandoning me to the challenges of adulthood? This thought is followed by a wave of gratitude. Unlike other teachers I've had, he sees my struggles, my brokenness, not as something to solve, something that renders any aspiration to goodness unrealistic, but as a matter of fact — something to accept and work with.

I leave his office and begin walking up Madison Avenue, and I remember a story he told in class years earlier.

> For almost an entire year, the young disciple Hanoch felt the desire to speak with his master, Rebbe Simcha Bunim — but he was too shy. Intimidated by the old teacher's gravitas, he kept to himself, avoiding the one man who he knew could help him as he wrestled with difficult questions. Finally, after many weeks, he summoned his courage and approached his teacher. He cleared his throat and said, "Master, I know what the commandments are, I know what the tradition teaches, but there is one thing I do not know: I do not know why I am here. What am I supposed to do with the life that I have been given?"
>
> The old master replied: "I struggle with this question every day of my life. Come — you shall eat the evening meal with me tonight."

I think of this story because, like the old master, Professor Wiesel didn't respond to my struggles with answers. Rather, he saw what I actually needed was someone with whom to share my questions, someone who would be with me without trying to fix things. More than anything, I realize, I need solidarity, the recognition of our shared, fragile humanity. I know I can talk to him, that it is safe, and that his insistence that I cultivate my inner authority, my own intuitions and wisdom, is right — though admittedly difficult. I didn't realize it at the time, but this theme became central to my life in the coming years, a kind of never-ending but still somehow joyful homework.

Toward a Methodology of Wonder

THE NEXT TIME I SEE Professor Wiesel is a few months later, at a conference in honor of his eightieth birthday. I have been invited to give a talk, and I am very grateful for the chance to share some of what I have learned from him.

I have chosen to speak about his approach to teaching and learning, a surprisingly under-examined area of his legacy. I decided to focus on this topic after discovering that there were only a few articles about this aspect of his life, though if you asked him who he was and what role he played in the world, he always answered: "I am a teacher." After years of observing him in the classroom, I've come to believe that, in spite of Professor Wiesel's inimitability as a person, his teaching methods can be taught.

I open with a rhetorical question: If we were to create an institute to train teachers and leaders based on the core design principles of Elie Wiesel's classroom, what would those principles be? In answering that question, I try to articulate a "methodology of wonder" that has the potential to awaken students' ethical and moral powers.

After my talk, Professor Wiesel nods at me and smiles. He is surrounded by well-wishers, so I don't approach him, I only smile back. But when I visit him in New York a week after the conference, the first thing he says is "It's a good idea!"

I'm confused. "What is?"

"Your idea for a teaching institute."

I realize that he has taken my rhetorical question seriously and wants to discuss it as a viable project. We begin brainstorming. He suggests I speak to administrators at Boston University to see if they will help fund such an institute, and he tells me he will call the university's president as well as some philanthropists he knows. He says, "Let's think about this. Maybe we can also do something at our foundation" (the Elie Wiesel Foundation for Humanity, which he and his wife, Marion, created after he won the Nobel Prize). I tell him that I feel strongly that we need to introduce more young people to his teaching and more teachers to his educational approach.

Our conversation continues, and we lay out a plan. But only a few weeks later, I see in the news that the Elie Wiesel Foundation has lost all its funds to a Ponzi scheme—a casualty of the infamous Bernie Madoff scandal. It is clear that our plans will have to wait.

Professor Wiesel publicly expressed his anger at Madoff, but the next time I see him, he greets me with an excited smile and says, "Come, come, I want to show you something!"

Once we are in his office he says, "I received this envelope from a young boy in Iowa. Inside was a five-dollar bill, and a note: 'I hope you make back all your money.' Look at what can come from something so bad."

"That's great," I say, "but can you really be so positive about this?"

He says, "It's only money. And anyway, for most of my life, if something bad happens to me, I close my eyes and remember other times, and what seemed so bad is not so bad. It's the same when something good happens. I close my eyes, and what seemed so good is not so good."

His perspective reminds me there is a bigger picture: whatever challenges I am dealing with will pass.

Beyond Celebrity

IN THIS PERIOD, Professor Wiesel appeared in the news often. In addition to his usual schedule of lectures given at universities across the country, his trips overseas, his speeches at the UN, and more, there were some new developments.

In 2006, he and Oprah Winfrey traveled to Auschwitz together. Oprah chose *Night* for her book club, propelling Wiesel's first book, with a new translation by his wife and partner, Marion Wiesel, to renewed prominence. Through the visit to Auschwitz, the two became close friends, and Wiesel appeared on Oprah's *SuperSoul Sunday* show several times in the ensuing years.

In June of 2008, he co-convened the fourth in a series of gatherings of Nobel laureates in Petra, Jordan, to discuss a range of issues: global economic development, media, the role of the arts, and, especially, hunger. Wiesel spoke of the humiliation of hunger and the ludicrous twin realities of global hunger and a culture of excess in first-world nations.

In 2009, he visited the Buchenwald concentration camp with President Obama and German chancellor Angela Merkel. The trip was Wiesel's idea, a way of cementing very publicly the memory of the Holocaust in contemporary American consciousness at a time when Iran was publicly engaging in Holocaust denial. During the trip, President Obama said, "We are here today because we know this work [of memory] is not yet finished. To this day, there are those who insist that the Holocaust never happened—a denial of fact and truth that is baseless and ignorant and hateful." He was referring to the Iranian regime, whose leaders publicly denied the Holocaust and even sponsored a Holocaust cartoon contest.

Elie Wiesel was now a household name among both older and younger people. *Night* had been a staple of high-school curricula for years, but with Oprah's endorsement, it was now an essential part of the American literary canon for a new generation. Elie Wiesel was a celebrity in the pantheon of secular saints like Martin Luther King Jr. and Gandhi.

But celebrity can eclipse the reality of the human being. It becomes easy for people to see the celebrity as an avatar of some general principle, an ideal, an abstraction. Professor Wiesel was a human being. He loved chocolate, was afraid of policemen, never learned how to swim, and didn't like celebrating his birthday. Those essential idiosyncrasies often get lost in the abstraction.

Worse, a celebrity can become an object of vicarious righteousness: *If I read the right books and listen to the right thought leaders, I do not need to take further action.* Professor Wiesel objected to such secondhand virtue and wore his celebrity lightly. Although he spent time with political leaders and, later, movie stars (whom he was happy to recruit to promote causes dear to his heart), he was more invested in his message than his image. He told me often that he still saw himself as the "yeshiva boy from Sighet," especially during public moments, when the cameras clicked and flashed. He would soon remind the world of his humanity again, this time through physical crisis.

Faith in Spite of All That

IN 2011, WIESEL HAD emergency open-heart surgery — a quintuple bypass — and later wrote a book about it, *Open Heart*. He told the story in public lectures and started conversations about vulnerability, mortality, and the mysterious process of revisiting old memories and beliefs later in life. In his new book he wrote, "In no way did I feel ready. So many things still to be achieved. So many projects to be completed. So many challenges yet to face. So many prayers yet to compose, so many words yet to discover, so many courses yet to give, so many lessons yet to receive." As a result of his deteriorating health, he had to limit his travel and reduce his workload. He stopped teaching his regular classes — the weekly trips from New York to Boston were too exhausting . . .

When I visit him, it's after the surgery and his recovery but before his new book has come out. I have never seen him so tired, so drawn. I am surprised by how old he looks. But he smiles when he sees me, seems to gather his strength, and becomes more animated as we speak. He tells me about the fear he'd felt when he was rushed into surgery and the premonition he had a few weeks earlier.

"I will tell you something strange, though maybe you will not think it's so strange. I went to visit the Belzer Rebbe" — a contemporary Hasidic master — "and when it was time to leave, he asked me, 'What blessing should I give you?' Without thinking, I said, 'A complete healing.' And this was before my emergency surgery!"

"You had an intuition?" I ask.

"I must have. Even when the doctor heard me describe my symptoms and told me to come to the hospital immediately, I didn't want to. I was meeting with a group of dissidents from Iran, and I felt that I could not interrupt that meeting, could not disappoint them. So I really had no idea. But sometimes we know things we do not know that we know . . ."

Then he tells me about a conversation he had with his six-year-old grandson, Elijah, soon after the heart surgery.

"My grandson came to visit me in the hospital. We sat together in silence for a while, his small hand in mine, and then he said to me, 'Papa, I know you're in a lot of pain. And Papa, you know I love you a lot.' Then he thought for a bit, and I could see him contemplating. 'Papa, if I love you more, will you have less pain?'"

I can see how moved he is by this philosophical comment, one that he himself might have made.

He says, "During my recovery I asked the nurse to move all the IVs from my left to my right arm as soon as possible so I could put on tefillin."

"Did that mean you had to get every single IV again?" I ask.

"Yes. It was not so painful. And I really needed to wear tefillin as soon as I could." (I remember that he had told me years earlier that the very first thing he asked for after the war was a pair of phylacteries.)

Then he tells me that when he was recently interviewed, the

interviewer mistakenly referred to his quadruple-bypass surgery.

"I corrected him," he says with a smile. "I told him 'Five — it was a *quintuple*-bypass surgery.' When I do something, I do it right!"

I am relieved to see his sense of humor is intact.

He asks me how I am, and I tell him that I am slowly realizing that my master plan — becoming an enlightened person while working full-time and being the perfect family man — is not going well.

My marriage has become complicated, filled with tension and misunderstandings. A combination of financial troubles, lack of time together, and very different ways of expressing ourselves has led us to a wall.

I don't really want to talk about this with Professor Wiesel, but he sees that something is going on and he presses me: "What else?" I speak haltingly, reluctant to burden him or maybe just ashamed of sharing this imperfect part of my life. But I do open up to him, and as I do I feel a little better. He has seen it all, and so much more.

He says, "Oy." He reaches over and takes my hand for a moment. "I am with you."

I am grateful that he doesn't offer advice.

I say, "I feel less optimistic in general than I did even a few years ago."

"This is a part of life. But this is also where faith, real faith, begins."

He thinks for a moment, then says, "You know, in the prayers we say '*v'emunah chol zot*,' 'and all of it is faith.' I changed it slightly. I say *'ve'emunah b'chol zot,'* which means 'faith *in spite of all that.*'"

"You say that?" I ask. Changing the text of the prayers is a theologically radical move for a traditional Jew, even if all it involves is an extra letter.

"I do, every day. Faith is in spite of everything, or it would not be faith. And remember the lessons of the Bible: Even the greatest leaders were flawed and made mistakes. That is okay. We are not supposed to be perfect; we are supposed to be human and, in our humanness, to become better, little by little. And you too—you don't need to achieve enlightenment. You need to learn to be happy."

I thank him, but I feel resistance to this message. I still want to be the hero of my life, to make everything work, to defeat the darkness. My idealism, my perfectionism, is still driving me, though I am beginning to wonder if it is also defeating me.

Then he says, as he has before, "Remember, your voice is as important as mine."

I have no idea why he is saying this now.

Then he says, "Ariel, there are very few things I wouldn't do for you, and if you ask me what those things are, I'm not even sure." He thinks for a few seconds and then says, "I wouldn't eat pork with you."

I start laughing, then he does too. I say, "I wouldn't eat pork with you either!"

We laugh for a few moments, then he apologizes; he is suffering from terrible back pain and cannot escort me out as he usually does. I say, "I wish you had told me; I wouldn't have taken so much of your time. Just feel better!"

He reaches his hand to me in lieu of a hug and says, "Come back in two weeks if you can." I tell him I will and then add, "Please God."

He decides, in spite of his back pain, to walk me out to the elevator. He is thinner than I have ever seen him. He embraces me and kisses my cheek, and I rest my hands on his frail shoulders. He says, *"Yishmirecha Elohim,"* which means "May God watch over you," and I step into the elevator. He has never said anything like that to me before.

The Gates Close

OVER THE NEXT MONTHS, as he undergoes various medical treatments, it becomes impossible to visit him. I try repeatedly, remembering his request that I come back in two weeks, but to no avail. The gates are closed, his privacy is being protected, and even those of us who are close to him, whom he invited himself, are on the outside.

I think about our most recent meeting, and I remember when he said to me, in a seeming non sequitur, after I told him of my marital troubles, "Your voice is as important as mine." I still wonder why he said these words just then. Now it occurs to me: Maybe he was reminding me that my personal challenges don't need to stop me from trying to make a difference. As I sit with this explanation, it feels more and more true, and it matches what I have been learning as I teach and sometimes counsel others: Our struggles often drive our greatest work.

Rather than repudiate those struggles, we need to claim them. This is an essential part of the homework Professor Wiesel gave me, and this is what I slowly begin to do.

I spend the next months focusing on this, using all the tools I have. I make art and exhibit it, occasionally selling prints of my work. I begin weekly therapy, exploring my formative years and how they affected me. I reconnect with a few close friends whom I haven't seen in a decade. I make sure to take each of my children on a road trip, to have time to connect more deeply. We go to Vermont, upstate New York, all over New England, and we find the best hot chocolate we can.

And I travel back to Israel and go to the Western Wall. Rather than pray in a subservient way, I argue with God. I begin with the usual prayer requests but slowly feel my back stiffening up, a sign I have come to recognize: I am faking it, going through the motions. And I become angry. Here I am at this holy place; I have traveled here for the right reasons, to reconnect, to find focus and clarity, and the doors are closed. "Okay," I say. "I've been here for almost an hour, and it's not happening. I'm going to take a break, and when I get back, I want something to open up—the wall, my heart, the heavens, I don't care what! I didn't come here to mouth pieties. I came here to find the center of my life again." Suddenly I am back in myself, inhabiting my experience, and I continue to speak out loud for several more hours, sometimes with anger, sometimes with angst, all of it with a new level of authenticity. I still don't really know what prayer is, but I am pretty sure this is the closest I have ever come.

· · ·

WHEN I RETURN FROM this trip, I get a message from Professor Wiesel's assistant that there is a slight chance I can see him in New York. I drive down from Boston, park, buy a cup of coffee, and call him at home. He sounds confused.

I tell him I've been thinking of him. "Why?" he says in a quiet, childlike voice. I tell him I am hoping to see him even for five minutes, to give him a hug, and he tells me to call again later. He sounds uncharacteristically distant, vague.

Later that afternoon I take a taxi across town so I can call from right near his home in case he tells me to come up. Finding a quiet spot to make a phone call in New York City proves to be a challenge; the traffic is loud, and there are few indoor spots where I can stand around for a while without being asked to leave. Finally, I find a lobby in an office building where I won't be disturbed.

When he answers the phone this time, he is his usual warm self, though he sounds exhausted. I don't tell him I am nearby because I don't want him to feel any pressure to invite me up. I am glad I made that choice, because he tells me that he has guests and can't see me. I ask if this is a bad time to talk, and he says, "No, let's speak for a little. What is happening with you?" I ask him to pray for my mother-in-law, who has just been diagnosed with cancer. He promises he will. He asks about my projects and then says, "If you need anything, just tell me and I will do it."

I say, "Really, I just want to see you. Can I try again next week?"

"Of course," he says.

I spend the day in New York City, at a bookstore and then

in Sheep Meadow in Central Park, a place where I spent a lot of time as a teenager. Beneath my favorite tree I take off my shoes and socks and allow myself to rest in the dappled shade. I let the sadness drain out of me into the bright spring air, the gently stirring grass, the serenity and openness of that large green window surrounded by gray city walls. I realize how much sadness there is at seeing my teacher in pain and at a loss for words. He once said to me, "All I have is my words," and another time, "All I am is my words." Now his words are receding.

Last Meeting

A WEEK LATER, in June of 2016, I travel again to New York. Elisha, his son, has set up this meeting, telling me, "It's important for my dad to see people who bring him joy." But Professor Wiesel has become so frail that a visit is not guaranteed. I arrive and sit in the lobby of his apartment building until he comes down. He is being pushed in a wheelchair by his nurse. His hair is thin and wispy, and he looks much older. But when he sees me, his face lights up. We sit in the lobby of the building, he in a wheelchair, I in a cushioned sofa, and speak for almost an hour. He makes me laugh out loud; that hasn't changed. At times I am able to make him smile.

We talk about so many things.

I ask him if he is writing. He says of course. I inquire about the subject but quickly interrupt myself. "Never mind, I know you never talk about what you're working on. What was the

last thing you wrote that you can talk about?" And he tells me
of a compelling reimagining of a Hasidic work, a daring literary experiment.

He asks me how I am, and I tell him that I am feeling that
I've lost time, that I've wasted it on things that weren't essential and that I am trying to make up for it now in a flurry of
creative activity.

He says, "Nothing ever gets lost."

"Nothing?"

I am thinking of how much he's lost. His father, his mother,
his little sister; the six million; and so many more across the
long years.

"Nothing," he says again. "It can take a hundred years, or
two hundred, or five hundred. We may never see it. But in
God's eyes, nothing gets lost." He seems to sense that I'm not
completely on board. "You want proof?" he says. "*You miss it*
— that's a sign that you never lost it."

He says, "Remember that I'm here, I'm always here for you."

I remind him that twenty years ago I asked him about faith
and doubt. "How do you teach faith and ethical awareness?"

He says, "I tried to teach all of my students love of learning
— learn, learn, learn. It is only through learning that we develop ethical awareness."

I say, "You succeeded with me and so many. But how do you
teach that?"

He says, "There is only one way — by *being* it. So people see
you and become inspired."

I ask him, "I am going to speak to many of your students.
What should I say to them?"

He says, "Tell them they're with me all the time." He says, "I feel responsible for every moment we were together." He says, "If not, why do we do it?"

I say, "There are some moments that become eternal. Your teaching is filled with them."

He says, "They are eternal because we were all present there together."

When I tell him that the challenges facing my marriage feel overwhelming, he says, "Ah—I was afraid of that. But you are learning, that's the main thing. That's what I always tried to teach my students, to keep learning, keep learning. I'm learning every day. I'm older than you, and I learn and learn and learn, and I still feel like I haven't even begun." He looks into the distance. "But I will soon."

When it is time to leave, I am not sure whether to embrace him. I am afraid of hurting him, so I reach out my hand and hold his for a moment. But he pulls me down to himself in his wheelchair, holds me for a moment, then kisses me on the cheek. His cheek is scratchy; for the first time in all the years I've known him, he hasn't shaved well. I move to get back up, and he says softly, "One more," pulls me back, and kisses my other cheek.

JULY 2, 2016, was a Shabbat. Since I don't use the phone or email on Shabbat, I might not have found out until Saturday night, when I usually checked the news for anything about Professor Wiesel. My friend Joseph, a local Reform rabbi, has a text hotline for congregants to let him know about deaths and other emergencies. He received a text saying that Elie Wiesel had passed away. Joseph walked several miles looking for me, to break the news gently. He didn't find me, but he did find my close friend David. And so when I went over to David's on Shabbat afternoon, he told me to sit down, and he gave me the news.

This shouldn't have been a shock, and yet it was. Professor Wiesel was eighty-seven, after all, and had been struggling with serious health problems for years. Still, my first thought was *He was so young!* I realized that for all his gravitas, his formidable presence, he was also childlike — innocent, curious, open. Although I had worried about him for so long, I could not imagine him gone.

That night I tore *kria,* the traditional Jewish response to loss. I cut the breast pocket of my favorite shirt, right over the heart, and cried.

I ARRIVE AT THE FUNERAL early after a long morning drive from Boston that I barely remember. I enter the synagogue and ask someone where the chapel is. I am told it's upstairs. So I start walking up the stairs, and ahead of me I see a procession from the Jewish burial society. They are carrying a coffin — my teacher's coffin. I escort him to the upper floor, then remain there, reciting psalms and speaking with him.

I remember the mystical teaching about the importance of the deceased person remembering his name. According to legend, a person who has just died must remember his or her name in order for the soul to ascend — the name is the key. But with the trauma of death, it is easy to forget. I don't know if I believe this literally, but I remember Professor Wiesel discussing it in class. So now, as people begin to trickle in for the funeral service, I quietly lean down and whisper, "Remember your name. You are Eliezer, son of Shlomo the Levite." Then I take my seat.

I listen to the eulogies from a distance. I still feel the wood of the coffin against my cheek.

TRIBUTES FROM WORLD LEADERS flooded in, most of them out of sync with the teacher I'd known. They described a modern saint, the world's conscience, an icon whose example had influenced millions. Though all this was true, I didn't recognize in their words the teacher I had known and loved.

Private messages from fellow students and friends were more meaningful to me. One wrote, *I'm a little directionless these days, trying to find words. I'm not succeeding too well.* Another: *Wherever he was in the world, we knew that his heart was always with us, in the classroom.* Another: *He was, for a time, so much my teacher—my priest, he used to say, only half-jokingly—and I am startled by the loss of him walking around in this world.* And another: *Somehow in my mind I felt convinced that he would outlive us all.* One student's words struck me especially. She wrote: *We are his legacy.*

A New Kind of Visit

A FEW MONTHS LATER, I visit Professor Wiesel's grave. No one else is there, and I have an hour or so to sit in silence and to speak.

What does one say in a moment like this? In *Open Heart* he

wrote, "The body is not eternal, but the idea of the soul is. The brain will be buried, but memory will survive it." Can he hear me? I don't know, but I speak nonetheless.

I tell him I miss him, that for every ounce of grief, I feel an ounce and a half of gratitude for our relationship. I tell him that I have a list of new questions, questions I regret not asking him when we sat together for the last time: How can I protect my children from hard truths without being dishonest? Which professional next step shall I pursue? What does he know about the Jews of the small village near his hometown of Sighet, where I have recently discovered I have ancestry? I tell him that I want to share his lessons with new students, that, as we face the final innings of a new and disturbing presidential election, we need his wisdom perhaps more than ever.

As I sit there, I think about our earliest meetings. I walked into his office wanting to be seen. I carried with me all the burdens I had always carried: my parents' divorce, my sister's blindness, my quest for transcendence, my many flaws, my search for love and purpose. He looked at me and smiled, elegant and accepting. With him I remembered myself and felt that I could become better, more awake, more responsible. I felt I already was those things when I was in his presence.

Suddenly I have an image of the first time I sat, a college freshman with a ponytail, in his office at BU. And I realize: There's another part of this story.

Professor Wiesel was an outsider, shy, obsessed with God, obsessed with ultimate questions, with madmen and beggars. He was a Hasid who knew asceticism like Americans know Starbucks, a man whose whole world—his family, his childhood friends and teachers, even the customs with which he was raised—was gone, all gone, taken away when he was a teen-ager, the time most people are beginning to form their iden-tities, however fragile and incipient. His identity was formed during days of forced labor, prisoner head counts, beatings, fe-ver, the separation from his mother and his golden-haired baby sister, and the death of his father. And yet: he was the sanest person I ever met.

He was always very thin, as if he never consumed anything more than the coffee and chocolate he loved. He had a far-away gaze but his eyes could also cut through you. His face carried evidence of time and suffering. He visited ashrams and "learned to listen to the stars." He lived half in ancient books and half in the *New York Times*, and he never apologized for be-coming a bridge between them.

He was not a joiner of movements, but he was akin some-how to the Beats and Essenes, the sadhus and dervishes and dancing Hasidim. He was an artist, a writer whose writing was a prayer, a pray-er whose language was silence. And laughter. I have the feeling that conformity wasn't ever an option for him. How could he even try to be like the others? His world had died. All he could do was live, read, write, contemplate, and find others—friends and students—who could accept his aloneness and maybe share in it.

I didn't know until recently that when he heard from my stepfather, Mati, that I had gotten into BU, he'd said, "Send him to me; I'll take care of him." I imagine that when he looked at me soon after that in his office, he saw a young seeker like him-self, bohemian, studious, sincere. I imagine he thought: *He's one of mine.*

I am someone who has often felt out of place, so that sense

of identification was a relief. Professor Wiesel provided me with shelter, a place and a spiritual context in which I could bring together all the disparate parts of myself. When he said to me, "Just be," he was challenging my tendency to perfectionism. This is a lesson I've had to learn again and again, ever since I told my father at age seventeen that I wanted to be a saint. It was Professor Wiesel who succeeded in teaching me where others had failed. He accepted his own and others' natures, gifts, and limitations. He accepted mine. Now I think that the best way I can honor him is to do the same.

As I sit in the sun by his grave, a sense of peace comes over me. I decide that it's time to renounce heroics. I want to be a human being, tasked with the slow work of becoming a little bit better, a little more sensitive, a little more open each day.

I often feel paralyzed when I consider the enormous suffering in our world. I've often let this paralysis stop me from taking even small actions. But now, I don't expect to find the perfect solution to the world's problems. I try instead to act in a way that might make a small difference—one person, one family, one classroom at a time.

PROFESSOR WIESEL ONCE told me: "To this day, if I have to make a decision in my personal life, I close my eyes and see my mother. I think, *What would she do?* If it's something which concerns the public, the community, I close my eyes and see my father."

Now I find myself asking, "What would Professor Wiesel do?" I continue to learn as much from him after his death as I did before it, and his words echo in my mind.

I think of his hands. I see the wrinkles on his face, around his mouth, at the corners of his eyes, on his lined forehead. The texture of his gray wool suit, the French Legion of Honor lapel pin always there, his thin legs in the suit pants. The wooden table in his office where we met, books everywhere. The way he held a pen to write, unlike anyone else I've seen, between the first and second fingers so his hand covered the place where he was writing. His scrawled notes. His warm and curious eyes, windows to a mind filled with fascination, with wonder. I know I will never be completely alone.

Postscript

WHAT DOES IT MEAN to be a student of Elie Wiesel? Does it mean standing up courageously against oppression? Does it mean traveling the world bearing witness to suffering? Does it mean becoming a fierce activist, disturbing the complacency of politicians and warriors alike, making the world a better place?

It might mean any of these things, but I believe it begins more modestly. I don't think Professor Wiesel expected all of us to act on the international stage, nor did he wish for his students to imitate him. You don't have to be a saint or the embodiment of an ideal. You don't have to have the word *humanitarian* on a business card. You don't need recognition or fame or great influence.

Being a student of Elie Wiesel means being yourself and cultivating your humanity, your sensitivity to others, in every moment.

It means noticing people at risk of invisibility, the ones without power or access, who also have stories to tell.

It means always learning, thinking higher and feeling deeper, always challenging yourself to dive into the great texts, stories, and ideas in search of wisdom.

It means asking questions and being comfortable not knowing all the answers, avoiding the temptation of premature resolution of complex issues. It means embracing mystery and knowing that we don't always have to tie everything up neatly.

It means knowing that you do not have to choose between your particular identity and your concern for all people, realizing that you can speak up for your tribe as well as for others, that the particular and the universal can be mutually reinforcing.

It means celebrating friendship, making friends with others who are searching too.

Most of all, it means remembering the past and understanding the link between past and future. It means choosing to care about others' lives, their suffering and their joy. It means becoming a witness.

ALMOST ONE YEAR after Professor Wiesel's passing, I am invited to give a lecture to a small group of divinity students on the topic of biblical faith and social activism. I decide that rather than give a traditional lecture, I want to open a discussion, using biblical texts as prompts, about the role of faith in modern life. The students come from different parts of the United States, but they all share a basically progressive orientation. We discuss the story of the Garden of Eden, the story of Abraham arguing with God, the story of Job. The students are fascinated by the idea that faith can be a kind of rebellion, a subjective art form, an act of affirmation in the face of and in spite of suffering. The students ask questions about how to lead faith communities in protesting injustice, and specifically about how to organize counterdemonstrations against far-right fringe groups. The discussion is supposed to last for one hour, but the conversation is so compelling that none of us realize that close to two hours pass. Fortunately, I have a little more time before I have to pick my children up from school.

As I'm getting ready to leave, one of the students approaches me with a serious look on his face. "I'd like to ask you," he says, "how can I cultivate faith when I just don't feel it?" I gently put my arm around his shoulder and say, "I've struggled with this for a long time. Let's sit down and talk about it."

Recommended Reading

THESE ARE WORKS TO which Professor Wiesel returned often or that feature prominently in the chapters.

Analects, by Confucius
Black Dog of Fate, by Peter Balakian
The Book of Legends, by Hayim Bialik and Yehoshua Ravnitsky
Brothers Karamazov, by Feodor Dostoyevsky
"Campo dei Fiori," by Czeslaw Milosz
Collected Tales, by Franz Kafka
Crime and Punishment, by Feodor Dostoyevsky
Darkness at Noon, by Arthur Koestler
Death and the Maiden, by Ariel Dorfman
The Death of al-Hallaj, translated by Herbert Mason
The Diary of Anne Frank, by Anne Frank
The Dybbuk, by S. Ansky
Elegy for Kosovo, by Ismail Kadare
Faust, by Johann Wolfgang von Goethe
Fear and Trembling, by Søren Kierkegaard

The Last of the Just, by André Schwarz-Bart

Life and Fate, by Vasily Grossman

"Making the Ghosts Speak" in *From the Kingdom of Memory*, by Elie Wiesel

Medea, by Euripides

Messengers of God, by Elie Wiesel

Mother Courage and Her Children, by Bertolt Brecht

The Myth of Sisyphus, by Albert Camus

Mythology, by Edith Hamilton

Night, by Elie Wiesel

Notes from the Warsaw Ghetto, by Emanuel Ringelblum

Open Heart, by Elie Wiesel

The Plague, by Albert Camus

Poems, by Anna Akhmatova

The Pope and the Heretic, by Michael White

Prometheus Bound, by Aeschylus

Rabbi Nachman's Stories, by Rabbi Nachman of Breslov

Romeo and Juliet, by William Shakespeare

Saint Joan, by George Bernard Shaw

Scroll of Agony, by Chaim Kaplan

Souls on Fire, by Elie Wiesel

Sula, by Toni Morrison

Tales of the Hasidim, by Martin Buber

Tao te Ching

The Trial, by Franz Kafka

The Trial of God, by Elie Wiesel

The Trojan Women, by Euripides

The Visit, by Friedrich Durrenmatt

Waiting for Godot, by Samuel Beckett

*We Wish to Inform You That Tomorrow We Will Be Killed with Our
     Families,* by Philip Gourevitch
The Yeshiva, by Chaim Grade
Yiddish Folktales, by Beatrice Weinreich

Acknowledgments

Many people contributed to this book.

Elisha Wiesel made my final, life-changing meeting with his father possible. I will be forever grateful for that, and for his and Lynn's friendship.

A book could and should be written about Mrs. Marion Wiesel, activist, survivor, humanitarian. She graciously shared her time and memories of her husband.

Many of Professor Wiesel's students and colleagues from different time periods were generous with their stories. I'd particularly like to thank Ingrid Anderson, Therese Barbato, Reinhold Boschki, Jan Darsa, Dan Ehrenkrantz, Carolyn Johnston, Marilyn Harran, Monika Kalina, Joe Kanofsky, Debbie Katchko-Gray, Roz Spier Kozak, Riki Lippitz, Aviv Luban, Jamie Moore, Nehemia Polen, Tina Rathbone, Bettina Reichmann, Pam and Jon Taub, and Yosef Wosk. It's an honor to be one of their fellow students.

Martha Hauptman welcomed me to Professor Wiesel's class over twenty years ago, and in doing so she changed the course of my life. Alan Rosen, Professor Wiesel's TA in an earlier era, is a wise teacher, a font of encouragement, and a fellow traveler along the Hasidic path. Stephen Esposito has been a teacher and friend from the moment Professor Wiesel sent me to his office to discuss his upcoming guest lecture on Greek tragedy.

Joelle Delbourgo, agent extraordinaire, told me in our very first conversation, "You don't need to look any further; I'm the right agent for this book." She was 100 percent correct. A lifelong learner, an insightful reader, and an effective doer, she guided me to the right publisher and editor.

Lauren Wein's connection to this book was immediate, personal, and unwavering, and her faith in it sustained my own. She is an editor-artist, and this book would not have been possible without her midwifery and magnificent guidance, from clarity of concept to impeccable cuts to final edits. She was able to hear my voice when I could not and to help it emerge.

Pilar Garcia-Brown, Tracy Roe, Lisa Glover, Taryn Roeder, Liz Anderson, Hannah Harlow, and the Houghton Mifflin Harcourt team are beyond impressive in their attention to detail, sense of humor, and unflagging enthusiasm.

Sara Sherbill, gifted editor, kind critic, and friend, pushed me to discover and then open new doors. Her presence throughout this project was an anchor. Her skill, precision, lucidity, and emotional insight enriched this book beyond measure.

Charlie Buckholtz, brilliant writer, fellow traveler, and soulmate since we met as teenagers, is my *chevruta* for the most difficult life questions. He applied the same humor, dexterity, and excellent intuition in advising me on chapters of this book.

David Jaffe is a firm source of support and clarity, someone whose Torah and integrity teach and inspire me every day. Joseph Meszler's sensitivity and friendship make my life, among many others', better. I will never forget his Shabbat walk on July 2, 2016, to find a gentle way to tell me the news of Professor Wiesel's passing. Both David and Joseph read early drafts of several chapters and offered insightful comments.

The staff of the Howard Gottlieb Archives at Boston University, where Elie Wiesel's papers are kept, helped me correlate my own experiences with his letters and other documents.

Emily Simoness of Space at Ryder Farm and the Levis family of the Wilburton Inn provided nurturing places to write, the first in 2008 as I was beginning to envision this book, the second as I was completing chapter 6. Harold Grinspoon, a visionary and a patron, Aryeh Rubin of Targum Shlishi, Gil and Elinor Bashe, and the Covenant Foundation, led by Harlene Appleman and Joni Blinderman, generously supported my work as an artist and writer.

My parents, Vivian Lazar and David Burger, supported my winding journey and partnered with kindness and devotion to raise my sister and me. Their friendship has been a source of strength my whole life. They are creative powerhouses whose legacy is kindness, curiosity, music, and the desire to teach. Mati Lazar was my mentor even before he blessed us by marrying my mother. He introduced me to Professor Wiesel and to the notion that it's possible, even today, to live with total devotion to the Jewish people. My sister Yaeli's strength and capacity for laughter and delight have always inspired me. My father's wife Sasha and my sister Silkie make everything sweeter.

Sabrina supported me in taking this leap, and many others, with love and courage: *Af al pi chen.*

This book is my way of expressing the profound gratitude I feel for Professor Wiesel's teaching, love, and support. It is dedicated to the children for whom I wrote this book so that they would know and be thirsty for more.

Permissions

A Conversation with Ariel Burger

How did the idea for *Witness: Lessons from Elie Wiesel's Classroom* come about?
In 2008, soon after I had ended my term as Professor Wiesel's TA, there was a conference in honor of his eightieth birthday, at which I gave a talk about his approach to teaching and learning.

It was astonishing to me that so much had been written about this great man, yet so little had been written about his role as a teacher, even though he always said that teaching was the most important public role he played. I wanted to address that lack, and to make it possible for many more people — especially younger people who wouldn't get to see him lecture or sit in his class — to learn from him. Professor Wiesel was very supportive of the idea, and we spent time discussing what I might include.

Elie Wiesel passed away while you were writing the book. How did that affect the writing?
Well, writing the book was already an emotional process. I felt so grateful for him, for my time with him, and for his message,

that I came to my writing sessions with a lot of enthusiasm. When he died, I couldn't look at the manuscript for a month. After that, I felt driven. I realized that now there would be no more lectures, no more classes, no more meetings. Not only for me, but for anyone. And I knew I had a story to tell, that I had an obligation, as all students do, to share what I learned from my teacher.

The themes of the book span many areas: religion, activism, art. Did you plan them before you started writing?
Some of the chapters' themes were clear to me from the beginning: I knew, for example, that there would be a chapter on faith and doubt, and one on song. Others emerged as I wrote. The chapter on activism, in particular, was in part a response to the new American moment of 2016, and on the erosion of civil discourse, the rise of hatred, the moral excesses on the far right and far left. I was always going to write something about Professor Wiesel's activism, but the current moment necessitated an entire chapter. All of this evolved through six or seven versions of the projected table of contents. The version I shared with Professor Wiesel in 2009 or 2010 is different, but still recognizable.

What do you hope people take away from reading *Witness*?
I want the reader to feel the experience of being in class with Professor Wiesel, to hear his voice and imagine his face.

I want the reader to know that he was a person of great wholeness and emotional range, that he was at times indignant about human suffering and the arrogance that causes it, that he could be pensive or funny. That his life went on after *Night,* and the corpselike face he saw in the mirror at the end of that book was not the end of the story.

I want us to reconsider categories like "faith," "rebellion," "madness," and to think more deeply about these categories. For example, one of the central themes of the book is that faith and doubt can coexist.

I want us all to feel that we can make a difference in a large and imposing world, that our inner resources are greater than we are led to believe. I want the reader to hear Elie Wiesel's message that it is our humanity that holds hope for our world.

What is the significance of the title?

At the center of the book is Elie Wiesel's teaching that "listening to a witness makes you a witness." That is one reason for the title, and it has a specific and universal meaning. Specifically, this is the response to the difficult question of what will happen when the last Holocaust survivor is gone: who will tell the story? Although no one who was not there can truly imagine the experience, we can absorb, integrate, and act as witnesses to their stories. In this way, as long as there are children and students willing to listen with sincerity and attentiveness, the reality of the Holocaust will never be lost.

More generally, we all come from somewhere: families, communities, stories of migration, religious or cultural traditions. We have the opportunity and responsibility to bear witness to the stories we've inherited. And I believe that it is by sharing our stories, rather than arguing about policy, that we can find our common humanity.

Elie Wiesel was a witness to the unimaginable events of the Holocaust, to the lost world of prewar Jewish life. But he was also a witness to the great potential of every human being to make a difference. He believed so deeply in education because he knew that it is possible for a person to change, to become sensitized to others' suffering, and to learn how to act to interrupt that suffering where possible. And when it is not possible to stop it, we can at least bear witness to it, so that those who suffer are not alone.

The title is also a verb, a call to action. My hope is that, through the book, readers will become witnesses to Elie Wiesel, as well as to their own teachers, traditions, and stories —and to one another's.

Discussion Guide

THE WORLD REMEMBERS ELIE WIESEL — Nobel laureate, activist, and author of more than forty books, including Oprah's Book Club selection *Night* — as a great humanist. He passed away in July 2016. Ariel Burger first met Elie Wiesel at age fifteen. They studied and taught together. *Witness* chronicles the intimate conversations between these two men over decades, as Burger sought counsel on matters of intellect, spirituality, and faith, while navigating his own personal journey from boyhood to manhood, from student and assistant to rabbi and, in time, teacher. In this profoundly hopeful, thought-provoking, and inspiring book, Burger takes us into Elie Wiesel's classroom, where the art of listening and storytelling conspire to keep memory alive. As Wiesel's teaching assistant, Burger gives us a front-row seat witnessing these remarkable exchanges in and out of the classroom. The act of listening, of sharing these stories, makes of us, the readers, witnesses.

Please visit arielburger.com for more information and to download additional materials, sign up for the author's newsletter, and learn about his availability for book clubs, talks, lectures, and workshops.

On Memory

"Is the sign that can prevent madness's ultimate victory . . . memory?" (p. 19)

Discussion question:

What did Wiesel mean by this? How can memory serve to protect us from madness?

Workshop question:

Share with a partner a memory that has shaped you. Talk about why and how this memory shaped you.

On Otherness

"It is the otherness of the other that fascinates me . . . What can I learn from him? What does he see that I do not, cannot?" (p. 51)

Discussion question:

What is the difference between tolerating and respecting the other? How does Wiesel's approach differ from the ways we often talk about difference and commonality?

Workshop question:

Wiesel believes that rather than collapse the distance between us, between our worldviews and opinions, we need to sustain the gap. We need to celebrate difference. Discuss ways in which you can do this in your own life. How can we work to see the familiar with fresh eyes, as Other?

On Faith and Doubt

"Believe me, if I had not had faith, my life would have been much easier. My questions are questions only because of my faith. My argument with God is an argument only because of faith. Sometimes I have wished to renounce it, but I could not." (p. 81)

"I believe in a wounded faith. Only a wounded faith can exist after those events. Only a wounded faith is worthy of a silent God." (p. 82)

Discussion question:

What does Wiesel mean by "a wounded faith"?

Workshop question:

What role does faith play in your life? What role does doubt play? How do you navigate the two? What might Wiesel's approach to faith and doubt contribute to conversations today about the conflict of religion and secular life?

On Madness and Rebellion

"One must be mad to believe that we can make the world better, that we can save humanity, or even a single life. It is unreasonable, irrational. But I am for that madness." (p. 114)

Discussion question:
Discuss the connection between madness and resistance. What are the varieties of madness? And how does recognizing madness help us to become "sane"?

Workshop question:
On pages 114–15, Burger offers us some of Wiesel's examples of different types of madness. Can you think of other real-world examples—from history or from current headlines? Or from your own experiences?

On Activism

"As we have seen, to turn away from reality, to pretend that evil is not evil, has one result: to empower evil." (p. 186)

Discussion question:
"We know that evil is at its most dangerous when it hides itself and tries to appear as good" (p. 180). Discuss what Wiesel means by this, and how we can work to expose the truth, so that we may call evil out for what it is.

Workshop question:
Wiesel urges that we take action ourselves, even if our acts are small and modest. We cannot pass this off to someone else, and we cannot wait for someone to give us permission. What are steps that we as individuals can take to resist evil? What resources or skills do you have—that others may not—that could allow you to make change for the greater good?

Beyond Words

> *"Sometimes, we must move beyond words . . . Teaching and learning do not happen only through the sharing of information; there must be an added element." (p. 190)*

Discussion question:
How does Wiesel transcend language? Why does he feel the need to do so? How does this help him communicate difficult ideas to his students?

Workshop question:
Wiesel has a profound love of music, and when he cannot answer a question, he sings a song (p. 208). What are some of the ways that you move beyond words? And what inspires you? How might you share these gifts with others?

On Witness

"All I have is my words."
"All I am is my words." (p. 244)

Discussion question:

What does Wiesel mean by these two statements? Discuss the ending of the chapter when Burger writes, *"I know I will never be completely alone"* (p. 252).

Workshop question:

Discuss what it means to be a witness. What are our duties as witnesses? How might you take the knowledge gained from your own experiences and share with others?